A Time for Every Purpose

A TIME FOR EVERY PURPOSE

Law and the Balance of Life

TODD D. RAKOFF

Harvard University Press
Cambridge, Massachusetts
London, England
2002

Library of Congress Cataloging-in-Publication Data
Rakoff, Todd D.
A time for every purpose : law and the balance of life / Todd D. Rakoff.
p.   cm.
Includes bibliographical references and index.
ISBN 0-674-00910-X
1. Time (Law)—United States.   I. Title.

KF450.T5 R35 2002
304.2'3—dc21
2002024079

For Dena

and

For Hannah

PREFACE

In the summer of 1965, having just completed my sophomore year in college, I spent a dozen weeks in Zinacantan, a Mayan village in the state of Chiapas, Mexico. As a junior member of an anthropological crew known as the Harvard Chiapas Project, I was supposed to help map out how Zinacantecos lived and thought, but my problem was this: I spoke English, a bit of Spanish, and very little Tzotzil, while most villagers spoke Tzotzil, a little bit of Spanish, and no English. I needed a study project that required very little speaking at all. Accordingly, I spent my summer living in villagers' homes recording, as precisely as I could, when they did what they did. The ways people use time, it turned out, form patterns that are at least in part constructed by the society in which they live.

I subsequently became a lawyer and law professor, and did not think further about time as a subject of study until one day in 1996 when I heard a report on National Public Radio about legislation pending in Congress regarding "flextime." What caught my attention was that, in a battle fundamentally between business and organized labor, women's groups were, according to the reporter, mostly siding with business. Here, I thought, is a phenomenon worth investigating. Fortunately my Dean, Robert Clark, agreed, and supported my plan to switch my summer research project to an unknown topic: "the law of time."

Six years later, I have written this book. Although it is entirely about conditions in the United States, it shows the heritage of both its parents. It is both about how our society shapes its use of time, and about the particular laws that participate in that shaping. I hope that it speaks both to the quest to understand how we live, and to the desire to decide what we should do to give a better shape to our temporal framework.

In those six years, I have been encouraged and helped by a large number of people. My colleague Daniel Coquillette was from the start a one-man cheering squad, sure when others doubted. Many other colleagues sent me clippings and references, and four—David Barron, Christine Jolls, Martha Minow, and Frank Sander—read and critiqued entire early drafts. So, too, did my Special Assistant Catherine Claypoole and my special friend Stephen Koster. The staff of the Harvard Law School Library and my secretary, Nancy Thompson, were assiduous in securing books and articles from all sorts of disciplines resident in all sorts of libraries. Two college buddies, Jon Boorstin and Stephen Poppel, each spent hours with me brainstorming possible titles. And several years' worth of Harvard Law School students pursued obscure questions on behalf of this book—among whom I should especially name John Golden and Kathleen Hartnett. To all of these friends and supporters, I can only say thank you. I certainly could not have written this book without your help. And I want to say an especial thanks to Professor Evon Vogt, head of the Harvard Chiapas Project, who had the true teacher's instinct to see that, even for undergraduates not destined to be anthropologists, field work in a foreign culture could be an eye-opening part of a general education.

CONTENTS

A Time for Every Purpose

1

THE LAW OF TIME

Sunday is more like Monday than it used to be. The Fourth of July is more like the third. Places of business that used to keep daytime "business hours" are now open late into the night. Schools in some communities are open throughout the year. And on the Internet, the hour of the day and the day of the week have become nearly as irrelevant as they are in the casinos of Las Vegas.

It is also true that most Americans still work less on the weekends than during the week. Trips and family gatherings are still scheduled around holidays. Yellow school buses are still more common in the winter than in the summer. And at any given moment, the clocks in Portland, Maine, still show a different hour than do those in Portland, Oregon, and individuals' lives are arranged accordingly.

The structure of our time is changing, and not changing, too. A half-century ago in the United States, most people experienced strong and definite dividing lines between days of rest and days of work, school time and summer time, work time and leisure time. Today the boundaries still exist, but they seem hazy and porous.

The law that helps order time is part of what has changed, and also part of what has not. The law in almost all states used to require labor to cease, or stores to close, on Sunday; in most, it no longer does. The law in almost all communities used to keep the schools open only during the fall, winter, and spring, and closed in summer; in most, it still does. And whether the work week should retain its legal limits, or whether it should become more "flexible," is repeatedly debated in Congress.

How should we, as a society, structure our time? Should we go even further than we have in relaxing the boundaries of time until we live in a world in which every minute is much like every other? Or should we sharpen some of the edges that we have let go dull? Or should we construct a new set of boundaries to shelter us from a formlessness that will make it impossible for us to balance the various time demands of our lives? And how should we use the law to pursue any of these goals? These are the questions this book attempts to answer.

Before we look at some possible answers—as we will throughout the book—we have to face the fact that these are not easy questions even to ask. Part of the difficulty is that we rarely recognize the "law of time" even when we meet it face-to-face. We know as children that we have to attend school a certain number of hours, a certain number of days, a certain number of years—but unless we meet the truant officer, we may well attribute this necessity to social custom and parental stricture rather than to the law. As adults we are familiar with "time-and-a-half for overtime," but less familiar with the fact that what constitutes "overtime" is a matter of legal definition. And when have we, when we turn the clock forward to start daylight-saving time, ever thought to ourselves: "Here is the law in action"? Indeed, this appears to be the first book ever written (at least in English) about the general subject of the law of time. But as we shall see, there is a lot of law that has a substantial impact on how we organize and use time: compulsory education law, overtime law, and daylight-saving law—

as well as law about Sunday closing, holidays, being late to work, time zones, and so forth. Once we begin to look for it, we will have no trouble finding a law of time to examine and assess.

However, there is an additional, much larger difficulty that inheres in asking a question like: "How should we, as a society, structure our time?" We do not ordinarily think of societies as constructing time at all. Time, we think, is an unformed, neutral backdrop that is just *there,* in which (or against which) activities take place.

Left to our own devices, we tend to think that time is natural, not social. Yet it is possible that we might not know any such thing as time if there were no social life. Some well-known scholars say the concept of time arises from, and is dependent on, social experience. Others say that our having the concept of time is innate, and that it necessarily precedes experiencing the flow of time. Fortunately, we do not need to take sides in this debate.[1] For what is clear is that even if there is a theoretical sense in which time is not socially dependent, time as we now experience it in fact depends heavily on how our culture organizes and uses it. In practical terms, whether we speak of the "social creation of time" or the "social uses of time," it comes to the same thing. We face time as a frame of our existence that has specific attributes constructed (or at least mediated) by the prior actions and concepts of our civilization.

The impact of socially created concepts can be seen even in the simplest use of time, keeping track of it. The day, for example, may seem to be nothing more than a name for a natural phenomenon caused by the revolution of the earth—nothing more until we ask what the boundaries of the day are. Within our own culture, we in fact have two answers to this question: "from midnight to midnight" when we are trying to be precise, and "from morning through the following night" for more casual purposes.

And both of these differ from the third possibility offered by the Book of Genesis, but not prevalent in our society: "And there was evening and there was morning, one day."[2]

The point is especially clear with regard to a unit of time that has no celestial referent: the week. We understand that what we call the "work week" refers to specific customs and institutional practices; but in fact the "real week" stands on no different ground. Nothing compels us to have weeks of seven days (other cultures have had different lengths), and indeed nothing compels us to have weeks. Yet as the sociologist Pitirim Sorokin wrote: "Imagine for a moment that the week suddenly disappeared. What a havoc would be created in our time organization, in our behavior, in the co-ordination and synchronization of collective activities and social life, and especially in our time apprehension. . . . We live and feel and plan and wish in 'week' terms."[3] What we take to be the "natural" way to think about time is in fact a result of cultural ingenuity.

This conclusion, however, still puts the point too passively. "Cultural ingenuity" does not just happen; it is the culmination of the efforts made by various people in various situations at various points in history to do things for various purposes, even if those purposes sometimes go awry. If we want to think about how we should structure our social time, we need to look at the matter in this positive, creative way. What can we, in our present situation, do with time? What purposes can we further by creating various temporal structures? How will the purposes of some of us fit with, or conflict with, the purposes of others? Once we look at the matter in this way, we will be able to connect the rather abstract idea that time has a socially created structure, with the quite concrete goals that others have sought to achieve, or that we might try to achieve, by organizing in one way or another the laws relating to time.[4]

Again, an example from the simplest use of time—creating the units in which we keep track of it—is instructive. Our understanding of the "hour" as being not merely a subdivision of the day, but a period of fixed duration, dates from the Western development of machines capable of keeping track of fixed durations—that is to say, clocks—in the fourteenth century.[5] When Japan was "opened" to the West in the nineteenth century, this system encountered the Japanese system of dividing each period of daylight and of darkness into six equal segments—a perhaps more "natural" system which had the consequence of making the Japanese daylight "hours" longer in summer than they were in winter, and nighttime hours the opposite. Subsequently, when the rulers of the Meiji government decided to pursue a policy of economic modernization, they adopted the Western clock as part of their program. They understood, as economic historians of the West would confirm, that having uniform hours was an essential basis for the exact calculation of time that supported Western methods of production.[6] They made a purposeful choice of which "hour" would be *the* hour.

Why do we, as turn-of-the-millennium Americans, do what we do with time? Probably the purpose that comes first to mind is not so different from that of the Meiji elite: we create time units so that we can count time accurately, and we count time so that we can know how much time is being spent. Time is a resource, a commodity to be directed to this use or that. The reason to put a form on time is so that we can allocate it in a planned and rational fashion. This view of time is embedded deep in our culture; it is, for example, the way of looking at things that underlies the analogy "time is money."

But even from the point of view simply of economic efficiency, a little thought will show that we need other structures of time beyond those used to measure it out. In addition to "counting time," we need to be able to "tell time"—that is, we need to place people and events in temporal relation with each other, so that we can coordinate what they do. Indeed, the careful coordination of the time of many individuals, so that their efforts are either synchronous or carefully sequenced, is a hallmark of production in modern societies. This point is most graphically typified by the assembly line, where lock-step physicality enforces lock-step temporality. Even in less obviously regimented jobs, and even with modern technology that allows a bit more freedom to "time-shift" tasks, the basic truth remains that the efficient functioning of our economy depends on a high degree of temporal coordination.

This is also true in endeavors other than business. Just as coordination is basic for production, once production has become a highly social matter, so too is it needed for the conduct of cultural life, civic life, and schooling, when those activities are carried out through substantial institutions. These institutions have to organize time to produce social capital just as businesses have to organize time to produce economic capital. And of course coordination is central to family life as well—and much more difficult to achieve for the modern family, which also participates in these other institutional frameworks.

The concepts that allow us to allocate time (our units of time) and to coordinate activities in time (the ways in which we "tell time") are only part of the story—for there are yet two more ways in which our society constructs time. Many of our time concepts (such as "Monday") repeat, and repeat with regularity. By making use of these concepts we establish rhythms which give to activities as diverse as going to church and going to work a predictable form and shape. Finally, we have some time concepts (for example, Thanksgiving Day) which are used to differentiate periods of time having distinctive qualitative features. Just as we arrange our physical surroundings so that certain spaces, such as parks, have special meanings in relation to other, contrasting spaces, so we can arrange our time so that certain times, such as holidays in contrast with working days, have a meaningful texture as well.

To put the matter more succinctly, when we as a society deal with time, we can construct time and use temporal concepts in at least four different ways: we can allocate time; we can coordinate activities in time (either synchronizing or sequencing); we can create rhythms through time; and we can create meaningful textures of time.[7]

Not only can we construct time in these many ways, but in fact we have done so and continue to do so. It is too simple to suggest, as some scholars have, that the modern history of time consists of an ongoing destruction of all situational features of time in favor of a purely abstract, commodified entity.[8] Rather, the history of time, taken from the rise of modern market societies and industrial production roughly two centuries ago, exhibits a progressive reorganization of time on several dimensions, rather than its mere abstraction. It is this history—to be discussed more fully in later chapters—that brought us the time zones and work weeks and school years that still set the parameters of our lives. And it is these structures that are being challenged by the developments of what some call the postmodern age in which we live.

Because we can purposefully construct time along multiple dimensions, the goals that we have when we think about shaping time are more complex than they might at first seem. Indeed, we can easily mistake what we want to do. We tend to think first, and often exclusively, of time as a quantity. "There's not enough time" or "If I only had more time": these are the ways in which we voice our grievances. But our real problems may not be matters of allocation at all.[9]

Consider, for example, the modern complaint: "There's no time anymore to sit down to dinner as a family." This might mean that father and mother, sister and brother, or some of them, only get 10 minutes to eat dinner, and necessarily have to eat it on the run. If this is so, the problem is indeed that not enough time is devoted to eating dinner. But it might be the case that all members of the family in fact spend 30 or 45 minutes eating dinner, but they do so at different times because of the demands of the other organizations in which they participate—the demands of jobs or of schools. If that is so, the problem, although put in terms of "There's no time," is not in fact the amount of time spent on dinner. Rather, the problem lies in the inability of the members of the family to synchronize what they do with reference to one another. The issue is not allocation; it is coordination.

Or consider this complaint: "There's no time to be a proper parent to my child." This might mean that a father or mother has so many other things to do—working at jobs, doing housework, caring for others, and so on—that he or she spends very little time with the child. If this is so, the problem is indeed that there is not enough time devoted to child-rearing. However, it may be that the parent in fact spends a lot of time with the child, but always in bits and pieces shared with, or snatched away from, other tasks that set the agenda. If that is so, the problem, although again put in terms of "There's no time," is not the amount of time spent on child-rearing. Rather, the problem lies in the fact that being with the child is always the second order of business, to be fit in when possible, rather than the first. Once again, the issue is not allocation; this time, it is control over rhythm and texture.

Now the law—to return to the special subject of this book—can be, if we want, framed to operate with regard to any or all of the four facets of time. For example, the law can require that an employee have a day off every week: that is an allocation of time to rest. It is a different thing for the law to require that an employee have the same day off each week: that is still an allocation of time, but it also establishes a weekly rhythm of rest. It is yet a third thing to require that all employees have the identical day off each week: that is still an allocation, still establishes a rhythm, but goes further and coordinates, indeed synchronizes, the time off of employees as a group. And it is yet a fourth thing to require that all employees have Sunday off: that includes the preceding three facets of time, but goes even further and creates a texture of time that incorporates a symbolic statement, religious in origin.

Or the law can leave matters like these to be decided primarily by the play of social forces and the agreement of private parties. There will still be a place for law—for instance, in enforcing the agreements parties do make—but it will have a more relaxed role to play.

The succeeding chapters of this book address these matters in three ways. First, there is considerable description: setting out the legal materials (ranging from statutes to Supreme Court decisions to the rulings of arbitrators) which have the greatest impact on how we, as a society, in fact organize and use our time. Here, we want to know not only what the law is right now, but how it got to where it is, and what the controversies are that might lead it to change in the near future. Second, there is the analytical dimension: considering what ways of thinking about particular laws best help us understand what is truly at stake in the creation, maintenance, or amendment of those laws. Since we have a tendency to think first in terms of the allocation of quantities of time, it will be especially interesting to find out what we can learn from looking at the other possible facets of legally constructed time. Third, there is the normative question: reaching a judgment as to whether the laws we have looked at are good or bad, solid or in need of change. Partly this judgment is a matter of the merits of individual rules: it is important to be as clear as possible about the choices and trade-offs involved. But it is also important to think about the overall structure of the law of time—what purposes the law of time usefully serves, and what form of law serves these purposes the best.

2

TELLING TIME

Wayne County, Kentucky, sits on the southern boundary of that state, a bit more to the east than to the west—pretty much due south of Lexington—and is located on the border between the Eastern Time Zone and the Central Time Zone. On October 29, 2000, the time changed in Wayne County. By order of the federal Department of Transportation, Wayne County moved from Central Time to Eastern Time; at any given moment, clocks now read one hour later than they used to.

Although the federal government acted in response to an official, local petition, sentiment in Wayne County was far from unanimous. In the contentious proceeding before the Department of Transportation, those favoring change had emphasized the county's commercial contacts with communities where Eastern Time already prevailed. Most of those who commuted to work outside the county went east, and most of the supplies for businesses inside the county came from the east, where the terminals for UPS, FedEx, and other carriers ran on Eastern Time. Opponents, by contrast, had emphasized the negative impact the change would have on farmers inside the county. Under Eastern Time, sunrises and sunsets would come an hour later by the clock than under Central Time; if farmers still worked by the sun rather than by the new clock, they would have trouble coordinating with other community activities. Some parents had pointed out that the schools' sports teams and other interscholastic activities connected the county's schools mostly with schools in the Eastern Zone, while others had emphasized the new dangers of waiting for school buses in the morning in the dark, if the time were changed. And of course there had been discussion of television: the major stations in the county all came from the Eastern Time Zone; but that, said the opponents of change, simply allowed viewers to see prime time shows, and the evening news, at a better time, an hour earlier. No one thought that the issue was more time or less time; the question was simply who would be able to coordinate their activities easily, and who would not. In the end the Department of Transportation sided with the proponents, finding that "it would suit the 'convenience of commerce' to move Wayne County from the Central to the Eastern Time Zone. Based on the facts presented, the county is very reliant on areas in the Eastern Time Zone to provide a majority of goods and services."[1]

What time is it? The mode for answering this question has varied several times in the course of American history.

Perhaps the simplest way of telling time is by direct observation of the sun: noon is the time when the sun reaches its apex. But the spread of clocks at the end of the eighteenth and beginning of the nineteenth century made direct observation obsolete for most purposes. And with this change, the time had to change, too. For, as a result of variations in the earth's declination and orbit, observable solar days—the time from one high noon to the next—are sometimes more than 24 hours, and sometimes less. Even though everything will average out in the end, observed solar time at various points in the year runs as much as about 15 minutes faster or slower than the time shown by an accurate clock counting out its 24-hour periods with mechanical perfection.[2] The averaged-out time that clocks show is known as mean solar time. By the middle of the nineteenth century, mean solar time was the standard way time was reckoned in this country; it was what people meant when they referred to their "local time."

However, as this phrase suggests, while mean solar time smoothed out the day-to-day variations in solar time, it was still based on the average position of the sun as seen from a specific place on the earth, and therefore varied widely from community to community. Because the earth revolves counterclockwise, at any given instant, the further east the viewer is, the further the sun appears to have traveled across the sky or, if time is figured locale by locale, the later in the day it is. Or, to put it the other way around, under the regime of local mean solar time the clocks in each community westward showed a few minutes earlier. (For example, mean solar time in Pittsburgh, at the western end of Pennsylvania, was about 19 minutes earlier than in Philadelphia, at the eastern border.)

This system of using local mean solar time worked pretty well so long as there was no need to know the time in any other locale with great precision. If it took several days to get from A to B, a few minutes more or less was not of great consequence.

What changed this was that great engine of social change in the nineteenth century, the railroad. Railroads could not operate on a time that changed from town to town; schedules and trains needed to be coordinated over broad terrains. Standardization was a matter of both safety and efficiency. With the aid of the telegraph, it was possible to have the same time displayed at every station, and so railroads began to run their whole lines, or large divisions of their lines, on a set time, usually the local time of their home offices.[3] The Pennsylvania Railroad, for example, ran on Philadelphia time all the way to Pittsburgh.[4] As a result, in many communities through which the railroads passed there

were two types of time—the local time and "railroad time"—and
there were two clocks in many railroad stations, one for each. At
railroad stations used by two train companies that standardized
on the time of different home cities, there might be three clocks;
at some major termini there were even more.[5] These clocks did
not vary by a uniform hour, as do similar banks of clocks in modern airports; rather, they varied in chaotic profusion by a greater
or smaller number of minutes.

Various schemes for a simpler system were put forward. Some
of these were still fairly local, such as Connecticut's passage, in
1881, of a statute making New York City time the legal standard
for that state.[6] In Great Britain, all the railroads had gradually
standardized on the time signal coming from the Greenwich Ob-
servatory, and this had led to a general standardization on that
time.[7] But Britain is much smaller than the United States, especially east to west, and accordingly the greatest deviation from solar time in their standardized system remained comparatively
small as well.

Scientists advocated for a national or even international system
based on sequential time zones. As a matter of physics, the
essence of time zones lies in the fact that the earth is both a
sphere and a clock. As a sphere, it is 360 degrees around, measured
by 360 lines of longitude called meridians. As a clock, it revolves
once every 24 hours. Putting together the earth's "sphereness"
and its "clockness," we see that in each hour the earth rotates by
15 degrees; or, to put it the other way around, we find that local
time differs by one hour at points on the surface of the earth 15
degrees apart. If we place the original line of longitude, the
"prime meridian," at Greenwich, England (as most maps drawn
in the nineteenth century did because of Britain's predominance
in world trade),[8] the meridian that cuts through the eastern
United States that will register the same minutes as Greenwich,
albeit five hours removed, is thus the 75th, which lies at the very

eastern end of Pennsylvania; the meridian one hour further away will be the 90th, at (to stay in the north) the western end of Illinois. Now, if we wanted to create geographic zones based on these meridians showing the least extreme differences between standardized zone time and local time, we would put the boundary halfway between them, along a nominal line of longitude 82.5. This boundary would run down the middle of Ohio. As we shifted from one zone to the next, zone time would change from being one-half hour ahead of local time—that is, time based on the 75th meridian compared to mean solar time as computed at the boundary—to being one-half hour behind it—time based on the 90th meridian compared to the same local time.

This conceptually pure idea might have appealed to late-nineteenth-century scientists; but the scientists lacked the power to alter entrenched local practices. Abstract rationality could not by itself break the hold of local time. A committee of the U.S. Senate, asked to consider international adoption of a time-zone system, reported in 1882 its view that "beyond the demands of the railroad traffic it seems absolutely necessary that local time shall be retained, because of the many industries and trade customs and legal questions involved."[9] Indeed, in the words of a leading historian of this subject, "only the railroads, the ultimate symbol of commercial expansion, progress, and the conquest of space, had the motive and the power to reform public timekeeping."[10]

The railroads in fact had more than one motive. They wanted to simplify the problem of scheduling. Most railroads kept a standard time throughout their own domains, or in the major divisions thereof; but since different roads standardized on the local time of different cities, this only exacerbated the scheduling of interline connections. There were, in the early 1880s, more than fifty different railroad times throughout the country, requiring numerous recalibrations at the junction points between roads or divisions.[11] Equally important, the railroads also wanted to simplify matters on their own terms.[12] If the country were divided up according to the scientific proposals, the time zones would start and end crisply along meridians of longitude that would bear no relation to where train trips might start or end, or crews change, or freight interchange. Substantially the same problem would arise if divisions were drawn according to the political imagination—at, say, state boundaries. What the railroads wanted was systematization on terms convenient to them: time zones with boundaries that matched functional interchange points, so that time would change between runs but would remain stable within them.

William F. Allen, secretary to the inter-railroad group that coordinated schedules, developed a zone map that fulfilled these desiderata. The time within each zone was based on the meridians counting from Greenwich: the railroad clocks throughout the first zone would show the time of the 75th meridian, five hours from Greenwich.[13] But the boundaries between the zones were drawn to trace the existing railroad junction points. (In the north, Central Time began, for example, at Pittsburgh.) The railroads adopted the plan and gathered (or coerced) the support of other important commercial interests. At noon on Sunday, November 18, 1883, the railroads by their own agreement established time-zone time. As so often happened in nineteenth-century America, what the railroads wanted, the railroads did.[14]

Of course, the railroads' action left open the question of the extent to which railroad time would become the standard time for the society as a whole. No substantial federal action was taken on the matter until World War I. The issue was fought locality by locality, state by state. Partly, of course, the general reception of railroad time depended on how much it varied from local time (or, as local mean solar time was now often called, "common time"). In Philadelphia, there was virtually no variance; in Boston, there was a 16-minute difference; in much of Ohio, it was nearly a half-hour. Partly, it was a question of attitudes toward the railroads.

Were they the exemplification of forward-looking technology, or the symbol of wayward power? And partly, responses varied according to more general attitudinal variations. Was it good to be focused locally, or was localism narrow and confining? Was it nature or man's scientific ingenuity that was to be preferred?[15]

These differences, as well as more technical legal questions, formed the background for the many lawsuits in which the choice between local time and time-zone time was litigated. The three most common types of cases involved the time to be used by the legal system in applying its own procedural deadlines, such as filing times for litigation; the time to be used in calculating the beginning or end of a period of coverage in an insurance contract; and the time to be used in figuring whether a bar or tavern had stayed open past the legally designated closing time. The decisions went both ways.

Two of the insurance cases show very well the contrasting arguments.[16] In Jones v. German Insurance Co.,[17] a fire insurance policy expired, by its terms, on "the 18th day of September, 1897, at 12 o'clock at noon."[18] On that very day fire broke out. The precise time at the site of the insured premises, in Creston, Iowa, was, in the words of the court, "at about 11:45 o'clock A.M. common time, or at about 2½ minutes after 12 o'clock standard time."[19] In other words, because Iowa was in the Central Time Zone but situated west of the 90th meridian on which Central-Time-Zone time was based, clocks registering standard time would show a later time, outside the insurance coverage, while those registering local mean solar time would still be within the covered period. The trial judge instructed the jury that they should presume that "common or solar time is the time intended by the parties" unless a different custom was shown.[20] Although there was evidence that Central standard time was used in Creston by the railroad, the schools, and businesses generally, the jury found for the plaintiff-insured, and the appellate court affirmed.

This decision favored local time not only by making it the presumptive time for construing contracts, but also by recognizing that proof of the custom of a business elite was not proof of the custom generally. It was not, said the court, that the railroads were wrong to adopt time-zone time. "Indeed, experience has demonstrated the inestimable importance to railroad companies of giving direction to employés everywhere on their lines of road with absolute certainty as to time. Without such certainty, safety would be imperiled."[21] And perhaps other business interests, allied to the railroads, found it convenient to use railroad time. But, the court wrote, "we are not quite ready to concede that, for the mere convenience of these companies, nature's timepiece may be arbitrarily superseded."[22] While it was true that observed solar time had to be converted to mean solar time to allow for the use of clocks, that "slight" alteration, said the court, had been recognized "for generations."[23] The sanctity of the natural, the force of custom, and the need to limit the power of railroads combined to limit the legal recognition of the railroads' invention.

In Rochester German Insurance Co. v. Peaslee Gaulbert Co.,[24] an amazingly similar fact pattern was presented six years later to the Kentucky high court, with the difference that since Kentucky was included in the Central Time Zone but was east of the 90th meridian, local mean solar time was later than time-zone time. Accordingly, the insureds argued for the application of standard time (by which the fire happened 15 minutes before the coverage ended at noon), while the insurance company argued for the use of mean solar time at the place of the fire, Louisville (by which the fire happened 2½ minutes after 12 o'clock). The jury was told to follow the local custom; they returned judgments for the plaintiffs (that is, in favor of standard time), which were upheld even though there was evidence that at least some businesses in Louisville still followed "sun time."[25] The language of this court, although phrased in terms of customary practices, was much more favorable to standard time than the Iowa court's had been. For one thing, the Kentucky court took judicial notice of the fact that "for the last 10 or 15 years . . . the custom has grown to be well-nigh general throughout the country to give the word 'noon' a slightly different meaning."[26] The court also relied on the argument that even pre-time-zone time was not natural, because it was based on mean solar time rather than direct solar observation. Thus, the new system was "no less arbitrary, but more fully meeting all the needs of society."[27] The evolution of time zones from being just "railroad time" to being "general social time" was not a forced progression to be resisted, but rather a natural social development:

> By establishing one uniform standard of time for all the territory within each of the sections named, a satisfactory, practical basis is attained. Business and social engagements naturally become adjusted to it. The custom originated, it is believed, with certain railroad lines in their endeavors to regulate the running of their trains which traverse wide sections of the country, so that unvarying and safe schedules might be adopted and enforced throughout a system where the average mean time was not widely different, yet was enough so to make danger in operating trains in different directions, on account of a minute or a few minutes' difference in the time of starting from the opposite extremes of the same line or section. Other business, including government and finally social affairs, adopted the same standards, until now it has become, in the more populous communities at least, almost exclusive.[28]

Of course, one might also say that these otherwise contradictory opinions share a desire to give protection to an insured party. Such a desire would have led the courts in different directions because the cases were situated differently with regard to the crucial meridian. But nothing in the opinions suggests that the courts were writing on such a narrow slate; nothing suggests that they would not each apply the same analysis to a similar problem on the boundary of the policies' times of initial coverage, where each analysis would result in a finding of no recovery by the insured.

Or perhaps the difference is simply a matter of the passage of six years' time, which made standard time that much more familiar.

Whatever might be said about these particular decisions, the effective resolution of cases like these, with their opposing sets of arguments, was ultimately signaled by Congress' enactment of the Standard Time Act of 1918,[29] which created five time zones (Eastern, Central, Mountain, and Pacific Time, plus Alaska Time). The Act reflected both the social origins of standard time in the actions of the railroads and the contemporary understandings regarding the appropriate role of the federal Congress. "The limits of each zone," said the law, "shall be defined by an order of the Interstate Commerce Commission, having regard for the convenience of commerce and the existing junction points and division points of common carriers." (To this day, as in the case of Wayne County, Kentucky, described earlier in this chapter, time zones are defined under the same legal standard, although now implemented by the Secretary of Transportation.)[30] Use of time-zone time was made mandatory only for the movement of carriers engaged in interstate commerce, and for the construction of any federal statute, rule, or order. But even though the states could still legislate a different time for their own particular legal regimes, the Standard Time Act basically ended the sway of solar time.[31] From this point on, the fighting issues were the boundaries of time zones and, as we shall see, daylight-saving time.

Time-zone time has become so basic to our perception of the world that it is hard indeed to imagine coordinating and organizing our lives without it. Sometimes this change of perception is thought to signal, because of time-zone time's denial of local time, the separation of time from space. But that claim of scientific abstraction hardly matches the contextual legal standard that Congress chose, with its reference to "the existing junction points and division points of common carriers" and more generally to "the convenience of commerce."

What might be more accurate is to say that the adoption of time zones signaled a reconfiguration of the social significance of particular kinds of space. Standard time represented not simply a preference for "coordination" generally, but rather for a particular form of coordination. For those who lived their lives locally, local time was as effective as time-zone time for arranging appointments, work schedules, school bells, and the like. For those who, in their occupations, had to coordinate with daylight, local time—local mean solar time—could in fact be better. Even for any one railroad company, operating solely on the time of its home office was sufficient to set up a schedule. Undoubtedly the basic driving force behind time-zone time, in the United States and elsewhere, was large-scale commerce—first in the form of mail carriages, railroads, and telegraph signals, and then more generally in the interconnectedness of economic systems as a whole.[32] It was the value of coordinating across large distances and many parties that the implementation of time-zone time confirmed.

The adoption of time-zone time not only accepted this view of social space; it furthered it as well. The very fact of sharing the same time, like the sharing of other basic suppositions of life, promotes solidarity; by contrast, having to translate time from one system to another makes difference palpable. (For this very reason the current regime in China, trying to knit together a highly differentiated land, insists on there being uniform time throughout the country despite its huge breadth.) In addition, the practice of coordinated cooperation also furthers social cohesion. When we adjust our actions to fit with those of others in a

continuous and organized way, we create both commonalities of
interest and understandings of the world dependent on continued coordination. Since the adoption of time zones promoted coordination over a larger terrain, it also furthered a broader view
of the society of which each individual was a part.[33]

Of course, the creation of temporal homogeneity within each
time zone comes at the cost of creating discontinuities at the
edges of the zones. Early on, there was a serious proposal to divide the earth into 10-minute-wide time zones, 144 in all.[34] This
was rejected as inconvenient. Had it been adopted, not only
would time-zone time have been much closer to solar time, but
the differences at the borders would also have been much smaller.
As we now have it, we can coordinate easily across large distances
within a single time zone, but we also have large differences at the
boundaries. A boundary that makes a large difference becomes,
of course, an important boundary. Activities that must coordinate across a zone boundary have to assume an added burden.
And with larger, more distinct time zones, the issue of which
time zone is primary becomes a symbolic matter as well. When
TV shows are scheduled to start at "x hour, Eastern Standard
Time," the distinction, and the implied hegemony, are clear to
those not on the east coast.

The zone boundaries established by the Interstate Commerce
Commission (ICC), effective January 1, 1919, varied somewhat
from the pre-existing railroad time: boundaries were made more
compact, so as to be more intelligible, and were drawn through
rural areas, so as to inconvenience fewer people. More broadly, as
directed by the statute, the ICC considered the needs of commerce in general, not just the railroads; commercial regions were
kept together.[35] Since then, there have been dozens of petitions
from various localities seeking to move across one or another of
the time-zone boundaries, such as the petition from Wayne
County, Kentucky, with which this chapter began. Many such re-

quests have been granted by the ICC or its successor, the Department of Transportation. The vast majority of changes have moved time-zone boundaries westward—or, to put it another way, have transferred communities to the zone to their east. This trend reflects the general orientation of business toward the east and the commercial advantage of being on the same time as those with whom one deals. The pull of this commercial motive can be seen in the fact that many of the changes that moved territory from Central Time to Eastern Time, in Michigan, Ohio, and Indiana, or further south in Kentucky, Tennessee, and Georgia, established a new time that was further from local mean solar time— less "natural"—than the time being replaced.[36] As the ICC itself summarized this history in 1960, "the boundary between the eastern and central zones has gradually been moved westward so as to provide a standard of time for points in the western part of the eastern zone generally 40 to 45 minutes faster than mean sun time."[37]

In general, these changes in the Midwest pitted business interests, who wanted to synchronize with the eastern seaboard, against those who were more interested in staying close to local mean solar time and who especially did not want to lose daylight from the morning hours: farmers and school boards.[38] But the alignments also depended on the particular context. When, for example, in 1936 Chicago officially (albeit unsuccessfully) petitioned to become part of the Eastern Time Zone (which would have put clock time 51 minutes ahead of solar time), the grain and livestock exchanges opposed the petition because they needed to coordinate with their producers who lived further west. "A difference of time between Chicago and the shippers of these agricultural products," said the ICC, "tends to make more difficult the satisfactory contact which leads the producer to ship to the Chicago market instead of its numerous western competitors."[39]

In addition to authorizing the ICC to establish time zones, the

Standard Time Act of 1918 also inaugurated daylight-saving time on a national basis. Under daylight-saving time, clocks are moved forward an hour; what used to be called six o'clock in the morning is now called seven. If we assume that the times at which things happen are not changed vis-à-vis the clock, one wakes up an hour earlier in the morning and goes to bed an hour earlier in the evening, vis-à-vis the movement of the sun, than one would otherwise do. Assuming that there are many hours of sunlight, which is to say, assuming that it is not winter, daylight-saving time thus shifts an hour of natural light from early in the morning, when most people would otherwise be asleep, to the evening, when they are awake. More waking hours are spent in daylight, which means that less fuel needs to be spent on heating and lighting than would otherwise be used. During World War I, England, France, Holland, and Germany all adopted daylight-saving time as a war measure to conserve fuel,[40] and after the United States entered the war, it did likewise through the 1918 Act.[41] The measure passed Congress with considerable support, and during the war, daylight-saving time was generally observed without much fuss.

After the war was another matter. Indeed, from 1919 to 1966, the legal enactment of daylight-saving time was a hard-fought political issue. Immediately after World War I, wartime national daylight saving was repealed, but only after Congress mustered the extraordinary majority needed to override President Wilson's veto.[42] Advocacy in favor of daylight-saving time continued at the state and local level, and it was enacted in some jurisdictions. In 1925 the Supreme Court sustained a lower court ruling that the federal Standard Time Act, as amended by daylight-saving repeal, applied only to interstate carriers and federal laws and instrumentalities; it therefore did not preempt Massachusetts' legislation that made daylight saving the local time of that Commonwealth.[43] A jurisdiction-by-jurisdiction patchwork resulted. On January 20,

1942, not much more than a month after Pearl Harbor, national daylight-saving time was reinstituted for the duration of World War II.[44] After this war ended, the patchwork resumed. Some states had daylight-saving time; some did not; some, unable to make up their minds, allowed each locality to choose; and among the jurisdictions that adopted daylight saving, there was no uniformity of starting or ending dates.[45]

This cacophony (or, rather, this chaotic "multitemporality") lasted until passage of the Uniform Time Act of 1966.[46] This Act, in addition to enlarging the number of official American time zones to eight (extending far into the Pacific Ocean), provided for a uniform national period of daylight-saving time.[47] States could not adopt another form of daylight saving; they could opt out of daylight saving as a whole, but only if the entire state (later amended to allow for the whole part of a state in one time zone)[48] did so. Since only Arizona and Hawaii,[49] and Indiana for that part which lies in the Eastern Time Zone,[50] have exercised this option, it may be said that the controversy over daylight saving has now come to an end.

It is hard to imagine that this much political wrangling was prompted by different views on the connection between daylight saving and energy saving.[51] A careful historical study of the debate during and just after World War I, set out in Michael O'Malley's *Keeping Watch*,[52] has shown just how much more was at stake.

Some of the debate was based on the symbolism of daylight saving. Daylight-saving time departs even further than time-zone time from solar time; moreover, its artificiality is concretized in the twice-a-year ritual of turning clocks forward or back. To proponents, this exemplified man's ability to use science rationally to plan society. To opponents, this was an affront to nature's (or God's) time, and it excited to some degree the type of nativist reaction that also opposed the teaching of evolution.[53] It was as if

Clarence Darrow and William Jennings Bryan had duked it out over daylight-saving time, too.

In fact, it might seem, at first glance, that the debate over daylight saving could *only* be about symbols. After all, the law does not make the doing of anything at a specific time mandatory; it only resets the background measurement. It is not illegal to reschedule all of one's activities to compensate for the changed clocks. If someone does not like daylight-saving time, all he or she has to do is wake up in the summer one hour later by the clock. Going to work from 10:00 to 6:00 per daylight-saving time is equivalent to working from 9:00 to 5:00 per standard time. And this works in the other direction, too. If someone wants to live by daylight-saving time in a place that does not recognize it, all he or she has to do is wake up in the summer one hour earlier by the clock. Going to work from 8:00 to 4:00 per standard time is equivalent to working 9:00 to 5:00 per daylight saving; there will be the same extra hour of daylight after work in the evening.

On second thought, however, more must be said. If the sole occupant of the universe wanted to work early and play golf in the long afternoon of summer, there would indeed be no need to reset the clocks; she would simply get up early, work 8:00 to 4:00, and report to the greens. But no one lives as the sole occupant of the universe. In an organized society, our golf player most likely has to work when other people are also coming to work, or when customers expect her to be there; and she most likely plays golf when other people are free to walk the course with her. Similarly, if cows will not give milk freely until after daylight, the solipsistic farmer can just wait and treat 6:00 A.M. daylight saving as his starting point, rather than 5:00; but the real farmer who has to make the 7:00 A.M. milk train (which in turn will not be moved an hour later, because it needs to get to the urban markets on time) has to start at 5:00 A.M. daylight saving and lose some of the production.[54]

In other words, what daylight-saving time is about, other than symbolism, is the way in which what each of us does coordinates—synchronizes or follows in sequence—with what the rest of us do. Because the coordination of activities in a modern society is so complicated, it can be safely predicted that, quite without legal compulsion, people's activities will in fact move with the clocks, rather than resist them. The economist might say that the transaction costs for individuals to resist the time changes are very large; the cultural analyst might say that the simultaneous and formal shift by most of the society changes what is seen as appropriate behavior. Whichever we say, a lot is at stake in deciding whether to adopt or abolish daylight-saving time.

It is, indeed, possible to identify specific lines of trade that historically have favored or opposed daylight-saving time. The makers and sellers of home gardening equipment and seeds were among the early advocates, on the belief that with longer evening hours of light, office workers would garden more.[55] Organized baseball, before the institution of night games under artificial light, also liked daylight-saving time; games could start later, and more people could get off work in time to attend.[56] Movie studios and theater owners, by contrast, got together in opposition to daylight saving. Fewer people go to the movies while it is still light out, and, to speak of a genre now nearly extinct, drive-in movies absolutely depend on its being dark.[57]

As a more general matter, daylight saving was most clearly attuned to the work patterns of the urban middle class. They rose later, were less tied to natural rhythms, and had a wide variety of recreational choices in the evenings. On the other side, farmers were strong opponents of daylight saving. They had to coordinate with the sun, but they also had to coordinate with what was happening in nearby towns and with transportation networks. Daylight-saving time, by increasing the gap between solar time and clock time, made this dual coordination increasingly difficult. This was especially true in the western ends of time zones, where the cumulative effect of time-zone time and daylight-saving time could create an hour-and-a-half, or even greater, difference between the clock and the sun.[58]

At least in the first go-round, the final balance of power was determined by the position of a third group, industrial labor. During World War I, Samuel Gompers and the American Federation of Labor had supported daylight saving. At the Federation's 1919 convention, however, the delegates, urged on by John L. Lewis of the Mine Workers, voted in favor of advocating repeal. Many unionized laborers started work early in the day, and had to get up even earlier because they could not afford to live close to work, or to have a car. They did not like their experience of daylight saving: they had to go to work in darkness, and the heat of the day lasted an hour later into the early evening, when they had to get to sleep. That daylight saving gave the middle classes a better way to spend their leisure hours was, in labor's view, hardly a counterbalancing claim in its favor.[59]

It is thus not surprising, given these conflicting forces, that wartime national daylight saving was repealed, and that the subsequent patchwork solution prevailed for so many years. Rather, we might ask: What is implied in the country's finally reaching a national near-uniformity? One possibility is that the balance of these forces has changed. It is doubtless true that the country is more urban and middle-class than it was in the early 1900s. However, that cannot be the whole story, because even on the eve of passage of the federal Uniform Time Act in 1966 there was tremendous diversity of state and local practice. In 1965, of the 50 states, 14 made no provision for daylight saving, 18 allowed local option, and only 18 had statewide daylight saving; of this last group, 10 were in the Northeast.[60] Even allowing for the fact that

in the early 1960s many state legislatures were still misappor-
tioned and thus overweighted rural interests, it surely cannot be
said that daylight-saving time was sweeping the nation.

As was made clear in the House Report on the legislation, the
primary motive for Congress to act on this matter was to establish
a uniform time that was easily reckonable; the fact that this uniformity could be achieved politically most easily on the basis of
adopting daylight-saving time was a distinctly secondary point.[61]

> The testimony [before the Congress] indicates that over the
> years millions of dollars and man-hours have been wasted in
> attempts to keep effective time schedules before the public.
> This problem, of course, is shared by bus operators, the rail-
> roads, and the air transportation system. Apart from this,
> but no less important, the traveling public, those involved in
> communications, those involved in commerce—in fact, vir-
> tually everyone who moves from one place to another, or
> has any contact with localities distant from his own—has
> experienced the frustration which arises from conflicting
> and confusing time practices.[62]

In the end, then, the same forces that led to the establishment of
time zones led to the triumph of daylight-saving time. The need
to coordinate with those at a distance, and to have a time system
that was easily reckonable across the nation, was deemed by law-
makers to be more important than the particularistic claims of
smaller communities.[63]

"The application of science to the means of locomotion and to
the instantaneous transmission of thought and speech have gradually contracted space and annihilated distance. The whole world
is drawn into immediate neighborhood and near relationship,
and we have now become sensible to inconveniences and to
many disturbing influences in our reckoning of time utterly un-

known and even unthought of a few generations back."[64] Thus wrote one of the progenitors of the time-zone system, in 1884. If we extrapolate these thoughts into our age, an age of increasingly global transportation, commerce, and communications—an age in which railroads are a symbol of what is slow rather than of what is fast—we come face to face with the question whether the entire world will eventually move beyond the time-zone system to become standardized on a single time.

This possibility is not mere science fiction. Universal time stated on a 24-hour (rather than a 12-hour) basis and standardized on the Greenwich meridian is already in use in circumstances in which coordination across great distances without confusion is the highest priority. It is known variously as Greenwich Mean Time (GMT), Universal Coordinated Time (abbreviated UTC),[65] and Zulu Time (so called because the time zone at Greenwich, the "zero" time zone, is known as the Z zone, orally communicated as "Zulu" to avoid confusion).[66] For instance, the air traffic control system works on Zulu Time (with the much-reported, if not so important, consequence that the computers of the Federal Aviation Administration hit Y2K—the supposed "millennium bug"—five hours "early" at 7:00 P.M. Eastern Standard Time, December 31, 1999). Universal time is also used by the U.S. military, short-wave radio broadcasters, international weather forecasters, and astronomers. It is the time system sanctioned by the International Telecommunications Union and broadcast by the National Institute of Standards and Technology from transmitters in Colorado and Hawaii.[67] And universal time is used—and we can expect to see it used increasingly—to set the time for international business exchanges, especially over the Internet.

We can distinguish two fundamentally different ways in which universal time might be used, if its use became general. It could function as a lingua franca, a code into which all participants translate their own domestic times in order to be able to communicate with one another. If a banker in New York wants to plan an important phone call with a banker in Tokyo, their stipulating the time as 1400 Universal Coordinated Time rather than 9:00 A.M. Eastern Standard Time both promotes clarity, in that the parties need know only their own translation into one general time (rather than into all the potential time zones around the world), and mitigates the cultural hegemony implied in the use of any one party's home time as the standard time. The virtues of this arrangement (under the rubric "cosmic time") were put forward as early as the late nineteenth century.[68] But the setup still represents, from the point of view of any participant, a two-clock system: local time and universal time. If what appears to be the current trend of history goes forward, we will have to consider the other possibility: that universal time might become the single and only clock we all use. We already have a world second and a world minute, in the sense that under the hourly time-zone system all clocks everywhere ought to show the same seconds and minutes; what universal time would do is extend this to a world hour and a world day. (And if we were considering truly cosmic time—time based on communication throughout the solar system or even beyond—we might even have to get rid of the day itself since its duration is, after all, a localism of our turning earth.)

Presumably there will not be much pressure to make universal time the sole time until quite a few activities are already synchronized by its use. Thus, we should imagine the question arising in a society in which many activities are specified by time-zone time and many others by universal time—a difference of up to eight hours in the continental United States, and more in Alaska and Hawaii. Moreover, the reason many activities have become timed by universal time is that they relate to complementary activities happening around the globe. The drummer whose beat they hear is an international, rather than American, drummer. Indeed, the claim for change will be based on that very fact: that it is parochial (both functionally and symbolically) to stay with local time when we have to coordinate with commerce around the globe.

Retaining our present system of time in those circumstances would indeed be parochial—but the question will be: is that good or bad? In light of the earlier discussions of time zones and daylight-saving time, we can see that maintaining a local time, which is what time-zone time would be by comparison to UTC, not only enables, but to some degree gives a priority to, coordination with those who are local with us. By contrast, universal time would be both a symbol of globalization and an enabler of it. As we have already seen, those who coordinate with others do not remain strangers; rather, they develop relationships and, if those relationships are systematic, they develop solidarity. Already existing elements of solidarity would be part of the very reason that those who were already dealing internationally would favor the adoption of universal time; we have seen the same mechanism at work in the various claims made by those who wanted to shift the time zone they were in, to mesh with those with whom they were dealing. But the connection is reflexive. Insofar as the use of universal time would promote a global sphere of cooperation, and give no priority to more local ties, it would become a constitutive element of yet further internationalization. Some would favor the development for precisely that reason. Others would doubt the wisdom of loosening our existing political and cultural ties to our local, state, and national institutions, in favor of connection to an international order run largely as an international commercial order.

But whatever one might think about globalization in this political sense, the degree of social and cultural adjustment involved in no longer coordinating at all with solar time—even to the limited extent that time-zone time does—is so large as to give one pause. It is perhaps no big thing to think of 12 o'clock on New Year's Eve happening simultaneously around the globe, whether in broad daylight or dark night (as was advocated in an op-ed piece in the *New York Times*).[69] It is quite a different thing to think of all children starting school at 8 o'clock UTC whether that is daylight or night, dawn or dusk, or of all of us going to bed at, say, 23 hours UTC regardless of the light. There are, indeed, people who already live in circumstances something like this—people so involved in international business that although they physically live, say, in Manhattan, they temporally live in Tokyo so that they can coordinate with co-workers or clients on the other side of the globe. But their very situation suggests the real possibility that the regime of UTC might be one in which powerful centers of commerce, in the name of coordination, force others to lead difficult lives. Of course, it is always possible to change the times at which things happen to compensate for the change in the measure of time; but the same could have been said of the adoption of time zones and of daylight-saving time. Indeed, the purpose for shifting the whole world to universal time as its sole time would be to some extent frustrated by such readjustment; and the lesson of history seems to be that it does not often happen.

We are, so to speak, situated between the sun and the Internet. Time—certainly the time of time zones and daylight saving—is not natural; it is a way of engaging with nature. Time, even the time of e-commerce, is not technologically determined; it is a way of engaging with technology.[70] The issue is not fated; the decisions we make will matter.

But in making these decisions, we need to keep clear what the time issue really is. The legal establishment of time-zone time, daylight-saving time, and potentially of universal time, too, shows as clearly as can be that the questions of what society should do with time are not necessarily issues about "how much time." These alternative systems of keeping time are human devices whose purpose is the coordination of activities in time, quite without regard to how much time is allocated to doing particular things. Moreover, the history of the controversy surrounding each new system shows that coordination is not a neutral issue. Who coordinates with whom affects people's material interests, their political organization, and their sense of the world. In short, coordination through the telling of time is a matter as ripe for the contest of politics and the purposive reasoning of the law as any matter of the allocation of time would be.

Yet, even though our system for telling time inherently incorporates policies that favor some and not others, no one favors deregulating time in this regard, if by deregulation we mean going back before the late nineteenth century to a system of "common time," that is, of local times closely keyed to the sun. We have accepted the law of telling time to such an extent that it no longer seems regulatory, but rather appears as simply a background condition of commercial and cultural life. A contract to work from 9:00 to 5:00 or a concert scheduled to start at 7:30 implicitly makes reference to this law. That we will have some such law is uncontested, even as we can see a new contest over its content rapidly approaching.

Few parts of the law of time are as straightforward, and as accepted, as those we have examined in this chapter. We now turn to a much more complex element of the law of time—indeed the most traditional of all legal measures regarding time—the establishment of rest days and holidays.

3

COMMUNITY AND FAMILY TIME

In 1692 the law of Maryland, then a colony, provided that "no person or persons within this province shall work or do any bodily labour or occupation upon any Lords day commonly called Sunday."[1] In 1957, more than two-and-a-half centuries later, the direct successor of this statute still made it the law of Maryland, now a state, that "no person whatsoever shall work or do any bodily labor on the Lord's day, commonly called Sunday."[2] In addition, the law provided, with some exceptions, that "no person in this State shall sell, dispose of, barter, or deal in, or give away any articles of merchandise on Sunday."[3] The constitutionality of these statutes was upheld by the United States Supreme Court in 1961.[4] Nevertheless, as we enter the new millennium, the law of Maryland now provides, with only a few exceptions, that people may work, and stores may be open, on Sunday as on any other day.[5] This story is typical of a great many states.

The law of time zones, which we looked at in the last chapter, does its work of coordination very much in the background. Even daylight-saving time goes unnoticed except for the days when we change the clocks forward or back. We now turn to the very different laws that govern Sundays and holidays. These laws announce as publicly as possible that their purpose is to change the contours of social time.

Indeed, it may fairly be said that over the long course of history, the law's endeavor to regulate the Sabbath has been the most striking legal effort to structure time. Recognizing a Sabbath day has, of course, been religious law for some sects since biblical times. On the secular side, Sunday had no special significance for the judge-made common law, but, by statute, observance of the Sabbath has been law in this country since the colonial period. In some colonies, church attendance was itself compulsory; in most, the law forbade sports, travel, or work on Sunday.[6] Stripped of provisions requiring church attendance, "Common Day of Rest" statutes were reenacted (or enacted for the first time in the newer states) into the twentieth century. They are often called "Blue Laws"—some say because of the color of the paper on which they were printed in colonial times, others because blue was taken as the color of fidelity to principle.[7]

It is hard to give a general picture of the Blue Laws because they varied substantially from state to state. It is also true that they were not always enforced with the rigor that they had on paper. But a compilation prepared as part of the Supreme Court's consideration of Maryland's statute in 1961 provides a good baseline for analysis.[8] This showed that 49 of the 50 states made illegal on Sunday something that was otherwise lawful; only Alaska did not. However, in some states the restrictions were fairly trivial: Montana, for example, only prohibited barbering, a few forms of public entertainment, and the sale of liquor. Other states, for example Connecticut, began with broad restrictions on working and selling, but also allowed numerous exceptions, ranging from doing "works of necessity or charity," to selling newspapers and ice cream, to presenting various sorts of entertainment. And some states, such as Kansas, had broad prohibitions with few exceptions. Overall, concluded Chief Justice Warren, as of the middle of the twentieth century, more than 40 states possessed "a relatively comprehensive system" of Sunday regulation.[9] Justice Frankfurter, focusing more particularly on the two core points, the cessation of work and of commerce, wrote that "thirty-four jurisdictions broadly ban Sunday labor, or the employment of labor, or selling or keeping open for sale, or some two or more of these comprehensive categories of affairs."[10]

What is the purpose of establishing the Sabbath as a day of rest? The Ten Commandments require one to "remember the sabbath day, to keep it holy,"[11] and go on to explain: "for in six days the Lord made heaven and earth, the sea, and all that is in them, and rested the seventh day; therefore the Lord blessed the sabbath day and hallowed it."[12] On this view, the believer, by resting on the Sabbath, participates in God's holiness by recapitulating the weekly rhythm of the Creation.[13]

Needless to say, this proposition represents a very particular view of the human condition. That is not accidental; throughout history and across cultures, societies have established and differentiated themselves by their distinctive shapings of time. Weeks are not natural; they are socially created. Weeks—if by that we mean the shortest period of time longer than a day in which the fundamental tasks of a society (most often, the holding of markets) are repeated—have been in some cultures three days long, in others five, in some ten, in others twelve, and so on.[14] Our own week of seven days can be traced to both Judaic and astrological roots.[15] Early Christians kept the Jewish Sabbath on the seventh day of the week and also celebrated the Resurrection, which, according to the Gospels, occurred on the first day of the week.[16] Eventually they jettisoned the Saturday observance in large part to emphasize their distinctiveness as a group.[17] Just as the dating of events in Western civilization starting from "the year of our Lord" signifies the historical coalescence of that civilization and

Christianity, so, too, does the observance of a seven-day week with a day of rest on Sunday.

Anticlerical revolutionaries have understood this. For instance, the French Revolutionary calendar of 1793, probably most famous for the names of its months (Brumaire, Thermidor, and so forth), also stipulated ten-day weeks, with a full day of rest on the tenth day, and a half on the fifth. While the ten-day period reflects the fervent rationalism of decimalization seen in other Revolutionary edicts, it also had a more directly political purpose: in the words of its chief designer, "to abolish Sunday"[18] and thereby reduce the power of the Church. It would indeed be hard to keep the seven-day rhythm which is needed to observe Sunday faithfully while living in a society beating to a ten-day drummer—a society in which businesses were closed on the tenth day and on the afternoon of the fifth (and not otherwise). But the prediction of Bishop Gregoire to the reformers—"Sunday has existed before you, and it will survive you"—has of course proven true.[19]

Although the effort to label the whole society and differentiate it from others may have been, historically speaking, the most important function of Sunday, it would not provide a good present-day basis for maintaining the Blue Laws. The coalescence of the calendar and Christianity is a problem, not a virtue, from the legal point of view. And, of course, no one is proposing, law or no law, to change the number of days in the week, or to establish a different day in place of Sunday. The relevant issue, rather, is what is to be lost or gained from having a weekly day of rest in common.

This secular point of view does not necessarily contradict the religious one, however. A few pages further along in Exodus after the Ten Commandments, God, in telling Moses the various ordinances he is to set before the Israelites, has this to say: "Six days you shall do your work, but on the seventh day you shall rest; that your ox and your ass may have rest, and the son of your bondmaid, and

the alien, may be refreshed."[20] On this view, the believer, by keeping the Sabbath, participates not in holiness, but rather in maintenance of a social ethic of relief from work.

But the social policy is not as simple as the Bible suggests.
Clearly, there are grounds to justify legislatures in requiring that
all employees have time to rest: workers should not be overtaxed,
and employers who voluntarily do the right thing should not have
to face competition from those who do not. This rationale carries
over to the self-employed as well, because if they are in a competitive environment, they can rest easily only if others do likewise.[21] But these premises show only that there are reasons to
limit the overall number of hours per week that people work. At
most, they suggest requiring that everyone gets at least a complete day off each week. This is considerably different from saying that no one should work specifically on Sunday.

Perhaps the truth is that the only way to secure agreement on
this further proposition is to add a religious motive; if so, in a diverse society we must be wary. Or perhaps the establishment of a
common day of rest can be justified as simply an easily enforceable way to give everyone a day off: if no one should be working,
and no store should be open, it is easy to tell who is disobeying
the law. But it is also possible that there are additional positive
features inherent in establishing a common day of rest. Here, as
elsewhere in our consideration of the structure of social time, we
must examine not just the allocation of quantities of time to various activities, but other dimensions of the organization of time
as well.

Indeed, Blue Laws implicate all of the several facets of time.
They of course establish an allocation of time. Six-sevenths of the
week belongs to one kind of activity, one-seventh to another.
They create a basic social synchronization within time. Each
worker performs activities of a certain sort—whether work or
rest—within the same time frame that others do. They set in mo-

tion a rhythm for time. Some of life's most fundamental activities, both at work and at play—not just Sunday, but also Monday morning and Saturday night—repeat on a seven-day cycle. And they establish contrasting textures for time. Whether we call it a difference between noisy time and quiet time, or between work time and leisure time (but, on the secular view, not between sacred time and profane time), it is clear that time, as apportioned by these laws, assumes a qualitative, not merely a quantitative, aspect.

It was, indeed, the value conferred by these additional aspects of the Blue Laws that ultimately justified them in the eyes of the Supreme Court, when they were challenged as violating the prohibitions on state entanglement with religion embodied in the First Amendment. The case—McGowan v. Maryland,[22] decided in 1961—brought before the Court seven employees of a discount department store convicted of violating Maryland's Sunday closing law as it then stood. They claimed, in defense, that the law was unconstitutional because its purpose was to facilitate and encourage church attendance for the predominant sects, and to establish an atmosphere consistent with the sacredness of the day as those sects viewed it.[23]

Laws "respecting an establishment of religion" indeed violate the First Amendment.[24] And there is no doubt that the law of Maryland "established" Sunday. The question was whether Sunday, as so established, was an embodiment of religion.

Chief Justice Warren, writing for the Court, had no doubt that Blue Laws were originally passed with religious intent; but, he said, they had now lost their religious character. The very exceptions to the prohibitions on work and commerce that Maryland allowed—for the sale of various sundries, the operation of amusement parks, and so forth—showed that the state intended to create, in his words, an "atmosphere of recreation, cheerfulness, repose and enjoyment. Coupled with the general proscription against other types of work, we believe that the air of the day

is one of relaxation rather than one of religion."[25] This legitimate
state purpose could not be served by the purely quantitative solution of giving each person an individual one-day-in-seven rest.
What was sought was "a day which all members of the family
and community have the opportunity to spend and enjoy together, a day on which there exists relative quiet and disassocia-
tion from the everyday intensity of commercial activities, a day
on which people may visit friends and relatives who are not available during working days."[26]

Justice Frankfurter, in an extensive concurring opinion, emphasized the impact of history and custom on the matter. History
showed the religious origins of the practice of Sunday rest, but
also showed its growth into a general social custom. In England,
Sunday "was a day of rest . . . in the sense of a recurrent time in
the cycle of human activity when the rhythms of existence
changed, a day of particular associations which came to have
their own autonomous value for life."[27] In the United States, as
Frankfurter's detailed rendition of statutes showed, legislatures
pursued not only "periodic physical rest," but also an "atmosphere of entire community repose."[28] In short, because Sunday
was established by law and custom as a day "whose particular
temper makes it a haven that no other day could provide,"[29] state
legislatures could continue to recognize this fact without creating
the establishment of religion forbidden by the Constitution.

Clearly the arguments of Justice Frankfurter, and even those of
Chief Justice Warren, have something of a bootstrap quality. The
law, for religious reasons, helps establish a customary practice
which is then used as a secular justification for later versions of
the law. Upholding the ensuing result has a particularly pointed
impact when the law is applied to those whose religious teachings
would lead them in another direction from the now-established
custom. This problem, too, was before the Court, in cases
brought by Orthodox Jews to protest the Sunday closing laws of

Pennsylvania[30] and Massachusetts.[31] If, to use the facts of the principal case, Braunfeld v. Brown,[32] Orthodox Jewish merchants had to close their businesses on Saturday by force of their religion, could they also be required by force of law to remain closed on Sunday? Or did this deny them the other religious freedom guaranteed by the First Amendment—the right freely to exercise their own faith?

Again the Supreme Court sustained the statutes. Sunday closing laws did not require anyone to confess against his or her beliefs, or to participate in any religiously forbidden practice. The harm was a loss of trade from having to close for two days, which Chief Justice Warren characterized as an "indirect burden on religious observance."[33] Imposing that burden was permissible unless it was gratuitous—unless, that is, there was another way for the state to achieve its aim without the imposition. The merchants proposed that Pennsylvania be required to allow stores to remain open on Sunday that closed on another day for religious reasons, as some other states' laws did. But the Court refused: that exemption, it said, could well undermine Pennsylvania's legitimate effort to eliminate generally "commercial noise and activity" from the day of rest.[34]

There were, it should be noted, dissenting voices in all of these cases. Justice Douglas thought it plain that Blue Laws represented an establishment of religion: "No matter how much is written, no matter what is said, the parentage of these laws is the Fourth Commandment; and they serve and satisfy the religious predispositions of our Christian communities."[35] Justice Brennan, with whom Justice Stewart agreed, did not think the laws established mainstream Christianity, but did think that the failure to allow dissenters to close on a different day was fatal. In his view, the economic harm to merchants of having to be closed on both weekend days was real, and its imposition required the states to come forth with a strong justification. Instead, all they had offered was "the mere convenience of having everyone rest on the same day."[36]

In order to see why the Court reached the decisions it did in these several cases, one needs to understand that by 1960 Sunday was no longer what it had once been. Dating back at least to the Civil War, there had been a mostly continuous, although contested, movement in which Sunday had changed from being a day only of worship and contemplation (the Sabbath in its Puritanical guise) to being a day of leisure (the Sabbath as understood not just by secularists, but also by more liberal religious groups). Much of the fight initially was waged over the appropriateness to the day of serious, but not religious, cultural activities. Public libraries in Boston, Chicago, Cincinnati, Milwaukee, New York, Philadelphia, and St. Louis for the first time opened their doors on Sunday between 1869 and 1873.[37] In 1891, the trustees of New York's Metropolitan Museum of Art, over the objections of its curator, began having Sunday hours.[38] More popular, yet still very respectable, activities followed along. The 1876 Centennial Exposition in Philadelphia was closed on Sundays; the 1893 World's Fair in Chicago was closed at first, but later opened on Sundays; by 1939, the New York City World's Fair not only was regularly open on Sundays, but held its grand opening on a Sunday with a dedication by Protestant, Catholic, and Jewish leaders.[39] Finally, ordinary entertainment followed suit. The National League authorized Sunday baseball as early as 1892, but it took some important baseball cities such as Boston, Pittsburgh, and Philadelphia until the 1930s to do likewise; meanwhile, by the 1920s Sunday movies were ubiquitous.[40] Over the same period of time the Sunday afternoon church service went out of fashion, while Sunday excursions and, later, Sunday drives in the car—and the Sunday sale of gasoline for automobiles—became commonplace.[41]

Against this background, any attempt to determine why numerous legislators in numerous states over a long period of time actually voted for Sunday day-of-rest statutes—or amended them, or failed to repeal them—would be futile. Certainly Sunday in 1960 was not the strict and dour day it had been. At the same time, historical meanings had not been entirely eliminated, and it seems hard to deny that in our society (in 1960 or today) to require Sunday closing and rest has in part a religious meaning. Chief Justice Warren wrote that "we believe that the air of the day is one of relaxation rather than one of religion," but his choice of the words "rather than" (instead of "as well as") probably represents his desire to distance the matter as far as possible from the First Amendment, not his assessment of the empirical truth.[42] The Court upheld the common day of rest as best it could. Underneath the denial of religious significance lies an appreciation of the social ingenuity embedded in this, indeed religious, invention. The rhythmic reappearance of a day with a different and valuable texture, synchronized for the whole community, was not, as the dissenters suggested, a "mere convenience." Gaining the common day of rest was worth the turning of a blind eye to the adoption of a religious point of view that it inevitably entailed.

That the synchronization of the day was the essence of the matter is shown by the Supreme Court's later decision in Estate of Thornton v. Caldor, Inc.[43] There, the state of Connecticut, as part of legislation that relaxed its general Sunday closing laws, stipulated: "No person who states that a particular day of the week is observed as his Sabbath may be required by his employer to work on such day."[44] The Court held this unqualified protection of Sabbath observance to be an unconstitutional endorsement of religion. It might seem strange that the government's choosing as a common day of rest the day that is the Sabbath of the majority does not constitute an establishment of religion, whereas its giving to each person the right to rest on his or her own Sabbath does. But what is missing in the latter case, precisely because the protection is so individualized, is any sense of general social benefit to be gained from the statute.[45] Or, as Justice Frankfurter had said earlier, in the McGowan case, "one-day-a-week laws do not accomplish all that is accomplished by Sunday laws. They provide only a periodic physical rest, not that atmosphere of entire community repose which Sunday has traditionally brought."[46]

We can perhaps best understand the significance of synchronization for the common day of rest by imagining its complete antithesis: by imagining, that is, not the absence of days of rest, but rather the existence of rest days spread evenly throughout the work week. Some people get Monday off, some get Tuesday off, and so forth, and no priority is given to any day even including Sunday. What would the consequences be?

In fact, we do not need to answer that question purely on the basis of our imagination. From 1929 to 1931, the Soviet Union carried out a similar experiment. For these two years the Soviets operated on a "continuous production week" which had two features: it was five days long, and one-fifth of the workers had each day as their day of rest. (The number of holidays was readjusted so that workers worked about the same number of days per year after the change as before.)[47]

The Soviet regime had two main purposes for this innovation. The first, part of its revolutionary fervor (and revolutionary insecurity), was anticlericalism. Like the French Revolution's adoption of a week of ten, Soviet adoption of a week of five days made it hard to go to church every seventh day. The second purpose, part of the regime's drive for economic modernization, was to achieve an efficient use of scarce machinery and industrial capital by working it not only day and night (for many parts of the economy had already been introduced to three-shift work), but *every* day and night as well. "It is completely natural that man must rest," said one of the chief economic planners, "but why must these mechanical slaves rest?"[48]

The supposed economic benefits did not develop. With a fifth of the work force absent every single day, it was hard to arrange meetings among managerial personnel during which all required employees were present. In production-line jobs, it was difficult to schedule workers so that a replacement was always on hand as workers continually cycled in and out of their ongoing positions. Workers, shunted from one spot to another, became less responsible for their work and their machinery. And machines, it turned out, could not be worked endlessly but rather needed frequent maintenance.

Perhaps these economic difficulties were a function of the state of economic development, both technological and managerial, of the Soviet Union in 1929, and would not play out the same if the experiment were tried today. The broader social consequences, however, are harder to ignore. When, to borrow the words of a leading chronicler of these matters, "the Soviet authorities essentially divided the entire society into five separate working populations, staggered vis-à-vis one another like the different voices in a polyphonic, five-voice fugue,"[49] they also created five separate populations for other purposes as well. Workers increasingly socialized with the 20 percent of the population in their time-cohort, and grew more distant from the other 80 percent. Clubs and cultural events were not what they used to be. It became more difficult to hold political or union meetings (not to mention religious services). Family life was disrupted, and although the Soviets were no defenders of the institution of the family, for practical reasons they had to start considering family requests for synchronized days off. But when they tried to arrange that, they found that it just complicated further the task of coordinating the workplace.

The resulting widespread disaffection combined with the economic disappointments to doom the continuous work week. In 1931 the Soviets went back to having a common day of rest (although, true to their anticlericalism, for another decade the day of rest was scheduled every sixth day, to maintain a six-day cycle).

Of course, we do not live in a command economy in which rapid and massive changes in working schedules are decreed by political officials. Yet we still face the same underlying structural issues. As a Labour member of Parliament argued during consideration of a Sunday closing bill during the 1930s in Britain, "I am not speaking as a Sabbatarian. . . . As a family man let me say that my family life would be unduly disturbed if any member had his Sunday on a Tuesday. The value of a Sunday is that everybody in the family is at home on the same day. What is the use of talking about a six-day working week in which six members of a family would each have his day of rest on a different day of the week?"[50]

Indeed, one wonders if the Blue Laws might not still have a use, when one opens the newspapers to find it proclaimed daily that we are on our way to the 24/7 working world. Of course, some industrial facilities, such as electric utilities, have to be kept running 24 hours a day, seven days a week, and some services, such as fire protection and hospitals, do, too. But when embraced as a general principle of the working world, in many respects "24/7" is simply modern jargon (minus the anticlericalism) for the Soviet Union's "continuous production week." A recent article on the front page of the *Wall Street Journal* seems to echo the voice of the Commissar when it explains the movement to 24/7 production in the tire industry as based on "the unspoken reality of manufacturing: Increasingly it is structured around the machines, rather than the people who run them. The reason is economics. Every hour a costly plant sits idle is a drain on a company's bottom line." As the article goes on to say: "Single parents, Little League coaches, students as well as preachers must contort their lives to meet their schedules, or give up things they love to do."[51]

The ability of workers to participate jointly in activities other than work is not merely a matter of individual happiness; it has important social consequences as well. Participatory groups build the skills and norms needed for trust, accommodation, and cohesion among members of a society,[52] and also provide the springboard for movements for social change. Groups do exist, of course, in which members each do their activities on their own time. But these tend to be rather passive affairs. The socially more valuable groups thrive on activities that the members do together. Blue Laws establish a common day of rest or, more precisely, a common day of non-work and non-commerce. These laws therefore favor those activities that are done in common and that do not relate to work or commerce: the activities of families, civic groups, sports clubs, political associations—and, of course, religious groups. Blue Laws do not force people to do things together; but they do provide an established time when people are free to do things together. They enable group members to coordinate with one another in a way that is much harder to arrange if there is not a synchronized day of rest from commercial activities.

Moreover, because the common day of rest appears weekly, so too can group activities adopt a weekly rhythm. When groups act in rhythm—when they do the same thing according to the same repeated time pattern—they tend to become more tightly knit. Social rhythms, say the anthropologists and sociologists, help constitute groups' consciousness of their own distinctiveness.[53] This, perhaps, simply states the obvious to those who have experienced strong family traditions of doing things together on Sundays or holidays. But what must be appreciated is that, while it may be true that solidarity creates a rhythm, it is also true that maintaining a rhythm helps create solidarity.

Finally, a common day of rest establishes a cultural gradient that gives meaning to the whole week and helps situate activities within it. We know on the personal level that Monday is what it is because it contrasts with Sunday, and that Saturday night would be very different if it were not predictably followed by a day of rest. But as a matrix for group activity, too, the emphasis on one day as a day of not-work and not-commerce, in comparison to the other six, serves as a cultural signal of the appropriateness of other forms of activity on that day.

This does not mean, of course, that the legal stipulation of a common day of rest automatically generates strong families, vibrant political communities, and active civic clubs. Self-evidently, the connection is weaker than that. But having a common day of rest does allow people to create such groups more easily, gives them some encouragement to do so, and makes it easier to reach out to add new members to the group. For a society which, unlike the Soviet regime, values voluntary group activity, in which the decline of family solidarity is widely decried, and which stands in danger of losing the "social capital" that grows from group involvement,[54] a common day of rest has substantial virtues.

Since the 1960s, however, there has been widespread repeal of the Blue Laws. Although some court cases have found various states' statutes so riddled with arbitrary exemptions as to be invalid,[55] most of this repudiation of the Blue Laws has been the result of legislative, not judicial, action. An exact description of the trend is difficult because it is varied: some states have removed most, but not all, of their restrictions; some have abolished statewide restrictions but allowed localities some option to differ; and some have differentiated between the prohibition of sales and the prohibition of labor in general. (In some states there remains a final vestige of the Blue Laws' religious heritage through continuing restrictions on the sale of alcohol.) Any "count" of current Blue Laws thus involves some interpretation. One author, writing in 1980, reported that 20 states still had statewide sales restrictions;[56] another said that as of 1984 only 13 states had statewide Blue Laws;[57] while yet another source claimed that, looking at statutes in force in 1985, 18 states restricted work in general and 19 restricted retail sales in general.[58] What is not in question, however, is that on any view, already by the mid-1980s the situation looked far different from that depicted by the Supreme Court in 1961. Since that time even more states (such as Maryland) have abolished most or all of their restrictions. As a matter of law, the common day of rest is now uncommon.

One is tempted to attribute this demise either to the growing secularization of our society or (perhaps somewhat inconsistently) to the growing pluralization of religious beliefs. Each trend probably helped to negate any inherent sense of the rightness of ceasing to work specifically on Sunday. But neither explanation is fully satisfactory, as is shown by the parallel denaturing of those other days of rest known as public holidays, most of which have no religious signification. Holidays, for better or for worse, are, like Sundays, not what they used to be.

The number of days recognized as federal holidays in the United States—in the sense that the President is authorized to issue a proclamation asking citizens to give appropriate recognition to the day—is enormous. They include, to mention some of those added in recent years, Carl Garner Federal Lands Cleanup Day (the Saturday after Labor Day; established in 1986),[59] National Pearl Harbor Remembrance Day (December 7; established in 1994),[60] and National Korean War Veterans Armistice Day (July 27; established in 1995).[61] The national holidays which have tangible legal effect, however, are few:

New Year's Day (January 1)
Martin Luther King, Jr.'s Birthday (third Monday in January)
Washington's Birthday (third Monday in February)
Memorial Day (last Monday in May)
Independence Day (July 4)
Labor Day (first Monday in September)
Columbus Day (second Monday in October)

Veterans Day (November 11)
Thanksgiving Day (fourth Thursday in November)
Christmas Day (December 25)[62]

Even these ten days have only a limited effect by federal law. Princi-
pally they are days off for federal employees, days on which federal
offices are closed, and days that do not count for the purpose of calculating various time limits in federal statutes or rules, such as court
rules.[63] Federal law does not make them into "national" holidays, if
by that term we mean widely shared days of not having to work
or of closing stores. This status they get, if at all, from state law.

States are not compelled to recognize the national list as their list
of holidays, nor are they restricted to it. For example, Martin Luther
King, Jr.'s Birthday was declared a national holiday by an act of
Congress passed in 1983,[64] but New Hampshire waited until the
early 1990s to recognize "Civil Rights Day" on the third Monday in
January, and only in 1999 gave it the title "Martin Luther King, Jr.,
Civil Rights Day."[65] More significant, perhaps, is the fact that states
are free to determine the legal effect of any recognition they accord
to these holidays. States can, for example, mirror the federal pattern
in state law; they can declare a state holiday and provide simply that
state employees get a day off, that various government offices and
schools are closed, and that various state-law time computations
are extended by the missed day. Closing the public schools can
have a substantial impact on the time system of the society as a
whole. But if the states do not go beyond the federal pattern, then
whether employees in private enterprise have to work remains a
matter of employer policy and private contract. (Almost all union
contracts provide for holidays on New Year's Day, Memorial Day,
Independence Day, Labor Day, Thanksgiving, and Christmas, but
they are much more varied with regard to other holidays.)[66]

Or the states can go further and prohibit all (or most) private
labor and commerce on holidays—treating holidays as, in effect,

additional Sundays. As a technical matter of determining the law actually in force in any particular state, we must, then, ask two questions: which (if any) holidays are given "Sunday treatment," and what does "Sunday treatment" now mean?[67] The states vary; perhaps one example will suffice. In Massachusetts, as of a recodification passed in 1962, Sunday was still Sunday: the law prohibited, though with many exceptions, both commerce in general and labor in general.[68] By the same statute, the national legal holidays (other than Washington's Birthday, for some reason) were also treated as Sundays: that is to say, the provisions of the Blue Laws were made applicable to them.[69]

Over the next three decades, both positions eroded. At first, stores were allowed to open after noon on Sunday (although not in general on holidays); meanwhile, New Year's Day, Columbus Day after noon, and Veterans Day after 1:00 P.M. were removed from Blue Law coverage, as was Martin Luther King's Birthday when it became a state holiday.[70] More recently, by referendum in 1994, it was established that "all stores and shops which sell goods at retail may be open at any time on Sundays and on Memorial Day, July Fourth, and Labor Day."[71] Thanksgiving Day and Christmas Day are the sole remaining survivors of full-day, required store closing in Massachusetts.[72] Otherwise, the movements to weaken the common-day-of-rest aspect of both Sundays and holidays have proceeded more or less side by side.

True, the case for the specifically patriotic national holidays might seem especially strong in that they could be said to emphasize, and help create, our participation in the large civic group which comprises the whole country. This virtue can be legally embraced; it does not raise the fears of establishing religion that Sunday closing does. (Recognizing Christmas, of course, is another matter.) But as the parallel movement of Sundays and holidays shows, it is probably a mistake to see the ideological content of the day as the essence of the situation. For while it is true that

Independence Day and Thanksgiving Day are full of national symbolism, it is also true that they are first and foremost holidays experienced with family, or fellow members of other groups. Especially in an era in which family members often do not live together, the recurrent reunions that holidays make possible are indeed important to continued family solidarity. Thus the decline of holidays, like that of Sundays, raises general questions concerning our attitudes toward work, commerce and leisure, social activities and individual consumption.

As we have seen, already by the middle of the twentieth century Sunday had become a day of varied recreation and leisure, as reflected in the many exceptions to coverage allowed in the statutes that generally forbade Sunday commerce. This situation could be stable only if the distinction between "leisure" and "commerce" could be sustained. But in a market society, some commercial facilities must be open so that people can use their leisure as they like; and once shopping itself becomes a recreation, what distinguishes going to the movies from going to the malls? As one recent historical treatment concluded, the Blue Laws "declined, in large part, because Americans wanted to go shopping on Sundays."[73]

To some degree this trend may have reflected a further decline in the religious objection to trading on the Lord's Day, or a growing diversity of the country's population. But large-scale structural social changes were also at work. For example, the development of suburban malls moved a lot of commerce from where people worked to where they lived, and thus to where they would be on the weekends. Even more significant was women's increasing participation in the work force, especially in the full-time work force. There were simply fewer consumers around during what used to be "ordinary" business hours. Sunday opening became more important to retailers, and less offensive to legislators, because there were likely to be many more shoppers to whom Sunday hours were especially attractive.[74]

These forces were translated into practical politics in large part through the adoption of a new attitude by large retailers, especially chain stores.[75] Whether abolishing Sunday closing, considered in the abstract, is good or bad for retail business as a whole is a debatable proposition: if having stores open seven days rather than six substantially increases the total volume of sales, it is good; but if sales remain the same, all that has been accomplished is to increase the cost of selling a static volume. There appears to be no conclusive evidence as to which of these possibilities is in fact the reality,[76] and large retailers, such as department stores, were often among the traditional supporters of Sunday closing. What seems to have changed is that large retailers became convinced that, whatever might be true of the impact of Sunday closing on the total volume of sales, large stores were losing an increasing portion of their business to smaller ones. This was possible because many state statutes either exempted small enterprises altogether, or exempted the kinds of merchandise often sold in mom-and-pop convenience stores.[77] (Today, of course, large retailers would also have to worry about widespread competition from always available e-commerce.) Because they could not eliminate these preferences in the statutes, the chain stores focused on repealing the laws altogether. In Texas, for example, retailers including Kmart, Toys R Us, Sears, and Walgreen ran a well-organized campaign, consisting both of lobbying and of generating "grassroots" support, that had a lot to do with that state's repeal of its Blue Laws in 1985.[78] In Massachusetts, yet more recently, large retailers including Bradlees, Stop & Shop, Shaw's, and Home Depot spent heavily to gain passage of a referendum question that abolished the last remnants of Sunday closing.[79]

Given this play of economic forces, the extent to which the repeal of Sunday closing represents "the will of the people" is a bit hard to say. Where repeal of the Blue Laws was put on the ballot, it succeeded only by narrow margins: in Maine by 52 percent to

48 percent, and in Massachusetts by 53 to 47, and that after considerable business spending favoring repeal.[80] At the same time, the trend is uniformly in the direction of repeal.

However, even if we conclude that Sunday and holiday restrictions on leisure activities, including shopping, have become anachronistic, that does not force us to reach the same conclusion about restrictions on Sunday work. Even in a service economy, the portion of workers involved in providing direct service to the consuming public of the sort that people want on Sundays is small. It would be possible to retain a prohibition on Sunday work and simply exclude from the prohibition all retail trade. Perhaps, in light of the availability of child-care coverage provided by the other spouse, some members of dual-career families especially want to work on Sunday. But there is little reason to think that the bulk of workers do. What, then, can we say about the general abolition, not only of Sunday closing, but of legal prohibitions on Sunday labor as well?

Even in the most traditional economy, some work must be done on Sundays. But in the course of the nineteenth century, with the rise of industrialization and of commercialized farming for the market, the amount of Sunday labor rose considerably (although, given a lack of data, we cannot say by exactly how much). The continuous production of the steel mills—to mention the example that was most notorious—was fed by workers who worked 12 hours a day, seven days a week. In response, Sunday laws in their guise as labor statutes were passed, repassed, and strengthened in the late nineteenth century (though often with exceptions for utilities and continuous industrial processes) in order to prevent the six-day work week from becoming a seven-day one. When, however, through union efforts, other legal changes, and further economic development, work weeks in general began to shorten and other rest time became available, the significance of specifically Sunday rest (and the additional ideological

impact that the importance of Sunday could give to labor demands) declined. The need for workers in the growing leisure activities allowed on Sundays also made not-working on Sunday
seem less special. These changes, to borrow the words of a leading scholar of the meaning of Sunday, Alexis McCrossen, "desta-
bilized Sunday's status as the day of rest." Legislation against
working on Sunday had, like legislation against commerce on
Sunday, apparently become an anachronism.[81]

Sundays (and many public holidays) are still legally established
through the force of public institutions which recognize them in
indirect, although important, ways. These range from keeping the
public schools closed to not delivering the mail. But, legally speaking, Sundays and holidays are unlikely to become again what they
used to be. There is no political impetus to make them so.

It is probably too soon to tell what the long-run social consequences of the demise of the Blue Laws will be. Historically, Mc-
Crossen says, other laws and practices regarding work, such as the
40-hour week, came to substitute for, and thus undermine, Sunday work legislation. But whatever may be true as a matter of historical causation, the question remains how complete and effective
this substitution is. For Sunday, and public holidays, do not represent merely the allocation of time to rest. They provide socially
coordinated, rhythmically recurring, qualitatively significant days
of rest. People need to rest; but they also need to maintain their
sense of balance by having stable and recurring relations with
others besides those they see at work. As a society, we need to develop and maintain the social capital provided by multiple constitutive social groups. Both of these things require more than just
minutes or hours; they require time with the kinds of structural
qualities that Sundays and holidays traditionally provided.

4

Work Time

In Massachusetts, not long ago, Johanna Upton sued her employer, JWP Businessland.[1] She was the divorced single mother of Geoffrey, aged 8, whom she cared for and supported. She was also a professional employee at JWP. When she was hired, she was told that her work day would run from 8:15 in the morning to 5:30 in the afternoon, with one or two days of later work each month. In fact, she routinely had to stay until 6:30 or 7:00, and she had a considerable commute. With the help of child care, she managed—until JWP's merger with another firm, Businessland, was announced. Johanna Upton was then told that, in order to help the company get ready for the merger, for several months she would have to work until 9:00 or 10:00 each evening, and all day on Saturday. She refused, and she was fired.

"Society," wrote her attorney in his brief, "accepts working parents, even working single parents. Society does not accept a single parent who abandons her child from Sunday evening to the following Saturday night. While there is a gray zone somewhere between requiring an employee to work seven days per week and the standard 9:00 to 5:00 Monday through Friday, . . . the conditions under which Ms. Upton was expected to work were clearly beyond the pale of what society expects or accepts for a single parent of a young child."[2]

But the court held that she had no claim for relief. Johanna Upton, said the court, was an at-will employee, which is to say, she could be fired for any reason or for no reason, as long as her discharge did not contravene public policy. That her employer had made informal representations about the hours she could anticipate working did not change that fundamental fact. "There is no clearly established public policy," continued the court, "which requires employers to refrain from demanding that their adult employees work long hours. Nor is any public policy directly served by an employee's refusal to work long hours."[3] As for the plaintiff's point that the question was not merely one of long hours, but of other obligations, the court took a similar view. "There is no public policy which mandates that an employer must adjust its expectations, based on a case-by-case analysis of an at-will employee's domestic circumstances, or face liability for having discharged the employee."[4]

The court in *Upton* stated that as far as it knew, no other court had allowed recovery for an at-will employee in comparable circumstances, and apparently that is still the fact.[5] From that starting point, Johanna Upton's problem was that she did not have an agreed contract with her employer that specified and limited her hours of work. From a somewhat broader point of view, her problem was that she did not have the power to insist on such a contract. And from a yet broader perspective, her problem was that society did not offer her the protection she needed to be able to balance her work time with her other responsibilities.

Labor is, no doubt, the fate of mankind. The proper scope of work time is an important issue for any society. Whatever the Massachusetts Supreme Judicial Court may say, it is an important element of public policy that there be limits to work time, in order to make time for other activities. This is especially true for a society as focused on work as is ours.

It has been the legislatures, rather than the courts, that have recognized the need to provide a legal structure for work time. The fundamental statute regarding work time is the Fair Labor Standards Act of 1938 (often called simply the FLSA).[6] The presumption it establishes—that the normal work week is 40 hours long, and the sanction it mandates—that any longer time is "overtime" that must be compensated at one-and-one-half times the employee's regular rate, together constitute one of the great timing mechanisms of our society.[7] (This same law also sets the national minimum wage; but the overtime provisions apply even to those making in excess of the minimum.) Of course, as a legal matter the time-and-a-half-for-overtime rule applies only to those covered by the Act, and so the FLSA is the source of another social distinction in the life of modern American organizations, that between "exempt" and "non-exempt" workers. Another way to state Johanna Upton's problem is that, as a professional, she was "exempt" from the protections of the Act.

As we saw in the last chapter, the now-mostly-defunct Blue Laws had as part of their purpose providing workers with some protection from being overworked. In this particular role, historians tell us, the Blue Laws were supplanted by the political, legal, and social efforts that created the 40-hour week. The logic of the point seems plain: the establishment of the 40-hour work week took over from the older legislation the basic understanding that the week was the relevant unit for timing purposes, but increased the protection the worker received. Working the six-day week allowed by the Blue Laws meant, for anyone working full-time, working more hours per week than 40; or, to put the point the other way around, limiting employees to 40 hours a week gave them stronger legal protection than guaranteeing them one day of rest.

In some other respects, however, the Blue Laws were more ambitious than the Fair Labor Standards Act. They had a positive, and not merely a protective, purpose; their goal was to set a tone for the life of the society, at least for Sunday. This showed up, of course, in their containing prohibitions on commerce as well as labor. Moreover, although riddled with exceptions, in theory the Blue Laws regulated all who worked, rather than just protecting employees in need of being shielded from their bosses; managers and the self-employed were as subject to these laws as the poorest laborer. Finally, this positive purpose could also be seen in their shaping of time: time off was to be time off for everyone at the same time, rhythmically repeated every week, and meaningfully separated from the other six days.

By contrast, "40 hours a week" can be analyzed, in terms of the four facets of time, in this fashion: Most clearly, it is an allocation of time to work (or, to be precise, a limit on the allocation of time to work). It has no inherent coordinating effect; since there are many more than 40 hours in each week—168 hours, to be exact—there is no reason within the rule why any one person's 40 hours will overlap with anyone else's. The rule might further be described as incompletely rhythmic: it adopts the basic weekly framework of so many of our activities, but it offers no assurance that the 40 hours of one week will have the same shape as the 40 hours of the next or the last. Finally, it creates no special meaning for any particular hour or day. Thus, the FLSA cannot be viewed merely as a more generous substitute for the Blue Laws, but must instead be analyzed on its own terms.

Is 40 hours a week the proper allocation of time to work? There is no particular magic in the number 40; unlike the seven days of the week, we cannot even say that it was handed down at Mt. Sinai. And even if 40 is the proper number, does stipulation of work time by the week establish a good framework with regard to the other facets of time? We could, after all, structure work time more tightly (by the day) or more loosely (by the month or even the year). Does the 40-hour work week allow not only for the coordination of work, but also for the coordination of other vital, but non-work, activities? Does it help to promote important social rhythms? Does it represent a good balance of the significance we give to work and the significance we want to give to other meaningful activities?

As with the other types of social time discussed in this book, it is helpful in answering these questions about the legal structure of work time to begin with a review of how we got to where we are. Methodical, intense labor within a time frame sharply demarcated by the clock is not a natural phenomenon. The patterns of the use of time more typical of pre-industrial societies, in which human activities were often timed to rhythms of nature—in which, for example, fishermen went in and out with the changing tides—probably hold the better claim to being called "natural."[8] Even early capitalist craft activities, such as weaving cloth at home under the "putting-out" system, did not call for our present fixed schedules. In the words of one of the leading historians of this subject, E. P. Thompson: "The [pre-industrial] work pattern was one of alternate bouts of intense labour and of idleness, wherever men were in control of their own working lives. (The pattern persists among some self-employed—artists, writers, small farmers, and perhaps also with students—today, and provokes the question whether it is not a 'natural' human work-rhythm.)"[9] But the hiring of some people by others according to the time they spend, and the rise of large and complex workplaces where the efforts of many workers must be temporally coordinated, changed all that. By the late nineteenth century, speaking very broadly (there were, of course, many exceptions), the characteristic work week in the United States consisted of six 10-hour days (and the characteristic legal timing mechanism consisted of prohibiting work on Sundays).[10]

Efforts to establish by law the 8-hour day (which for most workers would have translated initially to a 48-hour week) date back to the Civil War. But even milder attempts at the end of the nineteenth century, to guarantee the limit of a 10-hour day to those who had to work especially long hours, were by and large nullified by the intense opposition of the courts. Probably the most famous case is the now-discredited decision in Lochner v. New York,[11] which on constitutional freedom-of-contract grounds overturned a state statute stipulating a maximum 60-hour week, 10-hour day, for bakers. Laws like these, said the Supreme Court in 1905, "limiting the hours in which grown and intelligent men may labor to earn their living, are mere meddlesome interferences with the rights of the individual."[12] The cases were not entirely uniform, but even a decision like Muller v. Oregon in 1908,[13] which upheld a state 10-hour law applicable only to female workers, indicated by its emphasis on what it considered to be women's special need for protection that a generally applicable law limiting work hours would not be sustained.

Nevertheless, tremendous change occurred, especially just before and during World War I. "From 1905 until 1920," write the leading authors on this subject,

> the average working week of nonagricultural workers plummeted from 57.2 hours to 50.6 hours. In manufacturing it dropped from 54.5 to 48.1—the rough equivalent of an eight-hour day, six days per week. In 1910, 8 percent of the nation's workers labored 48 hours or less per week; in 1919, 48.6 percent did. The proportion of workers laboring over 54 hours weekly declined from 70 percent to 26 percent during the same decade.[14]

These changes were in part the outcome of successful union organizing, striking, and bargaining.[15] Partly they resulted from the combination of political action and social reform known as the Progressive Movement. There was also the startling and highly publicized unilateral adoption of the 8-hour day (and the $5.00 daily wage) by Henry Ford, coincident with his introduction of moving-assembly-belt production. ("This is the length of time which we find gives the best service from men, day in and day out," he said.)[16] And the efforts of the Wilson administration, especially during the war years when the government was so deeply involved with the economy, also helped to extend the 8-hour day, six-day week pattern.

But then not much changed during the 1920s. When Ford made another startling move in 1926, abolishing most Saturday work, few capitalists followed his lead to the five-day week; nor were unions very successful in bargaining for it.[17] As late as the late 1920s, only a few hundred thousand wage earners worked a five-day week.[18] On the eve of the Great Depression, in 1929, the norm was 48 hours, or perhaps a few more, per week, spread over six days.

By 1933, 15 million people were out of work, and many more were working enforced short hours.[19] To many at the time, the problem seemed not temporary, but permanent: technological developments had made human labor less necessary, and the only way to provide a job for all who needed one was to share the work. This was the theory behind the most radical work-hours bill ever to come close to passage, Senator Hugo Black's bill that would have limited work to a 6-hour day, five-day week—the "30-Hour Work-Week Bill."[20] With some limitations regarding seasonal employees, this bill passed the Senate by a vote of 53 to 30 in April 1933, and was favorably reported out of committee in the House. However, it ultimately failed of passage, in part because businessmen feared that it would prevent the economy from ever returning to "normal" conditions, but in larger part because the Roosevelt administration withdrew its support. For Roosevelt and his advisers, the long-run goal was to get the economic "pump" going again, with greater demand, more work, and what they viewed as full-time jobs, rather than sharing out the existing, lower level of production.[21]

The political thrust behind work-hours legislation was instead incorporated into the National Industrial Recovery Act.[22] This Act provided for codes of fair conduct, governing a very wide range of issues, to be drawn up industry by industry. The process was often under business control. When the issue of working hours came up, businesses whose employees worked short weeks had an incentive to use the code-drafting process to limit the competition from plants that "sweated" their labor with unusually long hours, and to label that an unfair practice. But the drafters had little incentive to control the practices of mainstream companies. In most industries, of course, normal practice had collapsed from the standards of the 1920s. In manufacturing, the work week had dropped to about 35 hours a week; in mining, to 30; in construction, to 29.[23] The Roosevelt administration, under union pressure, tried initially to establish a norm of a 35-hour week, but this effort ultimately failed; the code drafters were unwilling to bind themselves to the immediate status quo. The upshot was that 85 percent of the NIRA Codes set work hours at 40 hours per week (albeit the 7.3 percent of the Codes that provided for more than 40 hours applied to 38 percent of all workers covered).[24] The 40-hour week became the accepted norm. Senator Black's bill remained on the legislative agenda, and indeed was revivified when the Supreme Court declared the NIRA unconstitutional in 1935; but the administration continued to oppose it, and placated labor by supporting other parts of its legislative agenda, notably the Wagner Act establishing the National Labor Relations Board.[25] The principal piece of work-hours legislation that was passed shortly after the demise of the NIRA, the Walsh-Healey Act applicable to work on the government's own contracts, provided for an 8-hour day, 40-hour week.[26]

This is not to say that the fight was over. When the Fair Labor Standards Act was introduced in Congress in 1937, the exact number of hours to be set as a maximum (as well as the exact wage to be set as a minimum) was left blank because of political differences between the President and Congress. Labor still wanted a 30-hour week, while business (after the demise of the NIRA Codes) was slowly increasing the actual number of hours worked per worker. Serious consideration also was given to having an administrative agency set hours industry by industry.[27] But the balance of forces was, in the end, about the same as in the earlier battles of the 1930s; hours were set initially at 44 per week, to drop down to 40 per week within two years.[28] Agricultural labor, whose work week had stayed at about 55 hours a week throughout the 1930s,[29] was exempted from the wages and hours provisions of the Act,[30] as were several other classes of long-working workers.[31]

If we ask, then, from the point of view of history, why the agitation for shorter working hours ultimately led to a rule of 40 hours per week, pride of place must be given to the very fact of the Great Depression. The sudden, cataclysmic shift from full (or nearly full) employment at around 48 or 49 hours a week, to a situation where millions were unemployed and those who had jobs in industry were working 30 to 35 hours a week, changed the entire scale of what seemed normal or abnormal, expected or oppressive. Next in importance was the insistence of organized labor, and some politicians, that the way to cope with this unprecedented situation was to cut hours further, to 30 per week, in order to share what work there was. Everything that happened legislatively, happened in some sense in response to Senator Black's bill. Another factor was the stance of business, which was unwilling to freeze in place even the existing 35-hour (or so) week, in the hope that good times would eventually return. Finally, there was the position of the administration, which favored—in this regard surely reflecting President Roosevelt's own instincts—the goal of more production, and therefore more work, instead of dividing up what was currently available. Whether Roosevelt's opposition to the 30-hour week grew out of a conservatism that led him to shy away from a potentially radical restructuring of American working life, or out of an optimism that led him to refuse to accept stagnation as the inevitable end of economic history, is hard to say.

Whatever the politics may have been, there was still a need to fit the Fair Labor Standards Act into a legal regime that required limitations on contractual freedom to be justified. Congress articulated two rationales. First, it intended the Act to stifle oppression by employers who would take advantage of their workers' neediness to make them work very long hours just to make a living wage; second, it wanted to protect decent employers from the ruinous competition of those other employers who would in this fashion "sweat" their labor. The recital at the beginning of the Act stated both points: "The Congress hereby finds that the existence . . . of labor conditions detrimental to the maintenance of the minimum standard of living necessary for health, efficiency, and general well-being of workers . . . causes commerce and the channels and instrumentalities of commerce to be used to spread and perpetuate such labor conditions among the workers of the several States."[32] This statement was not mere window-dressing; many (although not all) of the provisions of the Act exhibited the same approach in more detail.[33] Sharing the work, by contrast, was not a stated goal. Although the Supreme Court's attitude was in doubt—a symposium on the FLSA published shortly after its passage included two proposed Court opinions, one upholding the Act and the other striking it down[34]—the Court ultimately sustained the Act (and overruled precedent to do so) on the theory that Congress had articulated.[35]

Indeed, this understanding of the Act—that it was meant to define a point at which labor contracts became unconscionable to workers and unfair to competitors—fits well both with the fact that the Act also enacted a minimum wage, and with the central feature of the overtime provisions themselves: exceeding the basic work week put a bonus in the worker's pocket. Time-and-a-half meant that those who were oppressed would get, if not shorter hours, at least more money, while production with overextended workers would become more, not less, expensive. If work-sharing had been the principal goal of the Act, a flat outlawing of overtime, backed by a criminal sanction, might have made more sense than permitting overtime at a "price" that went to the employee. (This prohibition of overtime is in fact what Black's "30-Hour Work-Week Bill" had provided.)[36] Of course, the fact that overtime is extra-compensated has always meant that, from the point of view of controlling working hours, the statute gives a somewhat mixed message: it articulates a norm and then makes it profitable for workers (but not for employers) to exceed it.

Congress' legal justification for the FLSA made sense only because of the historical setting. Had the 40-hour week been enacted a decade earlier, when the average work week was 48 hours long, it would necessarily have seemed—and been—substantially redistributional. Given the actual circumstances, however, the 30-hour week was the redistributive proposal; the 40-hour limit did not affect the mass of workers to whom the Act was potentially applicable. It operated instead at the margins of the existing distribution of work hours. This is not to say that the Act was intended to have no impact. The early, admittedly rough, estimate of the Department of Labor was that the number of covered workers who were employed in excess of the initial norm of 44 hours per week was 1,384,000, and that the number would approximate 2,184,000 once the 40-hour standard, to become effective in two years, was used.[37] But this was out of a total labor force of several tens of millions,[38] and out of a pool of workers initially covered by the Act roughly estimated at 11,000,000.[39]

"40 hours per week" was not meant to reconstruct the life of the average worker or the average employer; rather, it was meant to mark the point at which the ordinary employment relationship ceased. The desire to share out the available work, and for that matter the possible constructive uses of leisure, were part of the long-term context, but these aims receded in the particular choice of 40 hours against a background of workers who were, on average, working less. The 40-hour week marked the point beyond which employers were exploiting workers, and thereby undercutting other employers in the marketplace.

Almost immediately, circumstances changed. With the coming of World War II, and with the relatively full employment the economy has generally produced ever since, working 40 hours a week ceased to be an anomaly at the far end of a statistical distribution. Instead, the 40-hour week, understood as five 8-hour days, became the norm, both in the sense of being fairly common and even more so in the sense of being the set-point against which expectations and social understandings were measured.[40] Many workers in mainstream occupations—neither the poor nor the "exempt"—worked at least somewhat more than 40 hours per week, and the overtime premium they earned became a way of paying for entry into a middle-class style of life. Working overtime, within limits, became for many workers a sought-after status, not an exploitative one; determining who got the opportunity to work overtime became a significant matter in labor-management relationships.

These changed circumstances seem to have put the Fair Labor Standards Act into a contradictory position. On the one hand, it has been very successful as a statement of national policy. The Act (along with state laws fashioned in its image) has greatly helped to solidify the 40-hour week as the social standard. On the other hand, the rationale for making the norm legally mandatory has been thrown into jeopardy. It would seem that the Act's main function is to provide that some workers get a bonus, while others do not. If neither group of workers is being exploited, or otherwise has a moral claim to society's aid, it is not clear why the setting of wages for overtime should not be left to market forces in the same way that the setting of basic wage rates usually is.

The flaw in this latter argument is that it takes the stipulation of the 40-hour work week, with time-and-a-half for overtime, to be a rule essentially about money. But it is not. It is essentially a rule about time. There is good reason to have this rule, or something like it, even in today's world. But the reason is not the one articulated at the time the FLSA was passed. The rationale for the Act must be reconstructed.

In the present day, the fundamental reason to set a legal limit to work time is to make time available for other important social activities. Time spent not-working is not properly viewed as mere "leisure." It is time spent raising children and helping spouses, time spent going to religious services and participating in civic groups, time spent forming political opinions and working as a citizen, time spent forming friendships and doing things with others, and, yes, some time spent doing nothing. These activities help each individual establish a balance in his or her life that work, taken by itself, cannot provide. More to the present point, they also accomplish things of vital interest to the society as a whole. Perhaps the marketplace could successfully equilibrate individuals' desires for their own leisure with their desires for more money. But all of these activities, except perhaps the last, require people to participate together. In a competitive market environment, limiting the hours of work for social and communal reasons like these requires collective action. It requires collective action in order to achieve a proper allocation of time to work and not-work, and even more clearly, it requires collective action to achieve the coordination, rhythm, and texture of time needed to make both work and not-work activities successful. These propositions—whose veracity will be more thoroughly examined in Chapter 7—form the modern basis for the Fair Labor Standards Act, and the rationale against which its specific provisions should be tested.

It is clear, then, that we must view the provisions of the FLSA in light of all four of the facets of social time. We can start with the question most directly posed by the statute: Is 40 hours a week, with overtime allowed if paid at the rate of time-and-a-half, an appropriate modern norm for the allocation of time to work?

Treated as an abstract proposition, it is impossible to say what the "proper" number of hours of work ought to be. From a functional point of view, it might seem that one could take all the production needed for the society, determine how many hours of work would produce that total given the current technology, divide that number by the number of workers, and derive at least an average. However, quite apart from computational difficulties, such an approach depends on the assumption that the total of the goods and services that a society wants can be specified. In modern societies, for better or worse, the frontier of desire advances in front of the boundary of present production. No set number of hours will give us what we want, since we always want more.

Another possibility is that our human capacities set a limit to our productivity. After some initial number of hours of work per day, we become less productive: we get tired or bored or angry. If we work too long, these conditions affect our work the next day, so it becomes less productive, too. Perhaps at some point our output per additional hour worked actually becomes negative: whatever we accomplish in that hour is less than what we lose through the reduced efficiency we suffer in the rest of our work. In that condition, reducing the number of hours of work would increase what we get done. There would be a natural point at which the output per worker was maximized, and in regard to hours beyond that point, it might be said that working them was irrational.

There is some historical evidence to support this argument. At the least, when the very long work weeks that typified some industrial plants in the nineteenth century—weeks of 12-hour days for six or even seven days a week—were reduced, the loss of production was often considerably less than management feared. When the steel industry, under considerable political pressure, finally went off the 12-hour day in 1923, the increased costs were much less than had been predicted.[41] But they were not zero. The long hours had not been totally wasted. More to the point, there is no basis for extrapolating from this historical experience regarding the efficacy of very long work weeks, to the 40-hour week. If there is a natural stopping point for productive labor, it seems highly likely that it is greater than the 40 hours on which society has settled. Of course, even if the marginal hour of work is productive, a fresh worker may be more productive; it may be more efficient to have someone else do the job. But trade-offs like that, dependent as they are on both the quantity and the quality of the available labor pool, are usually better made by market forces than by legal fiat.

If, failing to find a natural limit to work hours, we look instead for a purely conventional limit, it seems that there is much to be said for 40 hours a week. Or at least that has been the judgment of politicians. Good work, well-paying work, secure work—rather than more limited work—have been the goals of labor policy ever since the end of the Depression. In regard specifically to the overtime provisions of the FLSA, the history after 1940 (when the 40-hour week came into effect) consists, not of changes to the rule, but rather of its application to an ever-larger portion of the labor force.[42] Whatever may have been the rationale for (or politics of) the original list of exemptions from coverage, amendments over the years have greatly reduced them. Although at first the Act exempted a large proportion of those who worked in retail sales and service jobs,[43] revisions in 1977, and again in 1989, left only those in small shops or unusual circumstances (such as those working in seasonal recreational jobs) without coverage.[44] While the original Act did not cover federal, state, or local government workers,[45] amendments in 1966 and 1974 brought the large majority of those workers within it.[46] And so on. In a report based on data from 1990, the Department of Labor found that of the roughly 76.5 million employees subject to the overtime compensation provisions, about 28.5 million (or 37 percent) were covered as a result of amendments passed in 1966 or later.[47] At the same time, the fraction of all employees who are agricultural workers—still not covered—has greatly declined. By far the largest group now exempt from the overtime provisions of the FLSA consists of executive, administrative, and professional employees.

In short, Congress has continually (although not yet completely) broadened the applicability of the FLSA. Setting 40 hours as the point at which ordinary work time becomes overtime is the rule which workers have wanted to embrace, and to which they have been admitted. By contrast, although Congress held hearings in the late 1970s on proposals to adopt a 35-hour week, no action ensued;[48] nor has the recent, well-publicized adoption of a 35-hour week in France had much impact, at least as yet, on the U.S. legislative agenda.

But of course it is possible that this approach is insufficient. In a widely noted book published a few years ago called *The Overworked American*,[49] Juliet Schor put forward the proposition that Americans face a "time squeeze" because they now work too long. In 1969, by her estimates, full-time employees—not just those covered by the FLSA—worked, on average, 1,786 hours per year;[50] by 1987, the figure was up to 1,949 hours—an additional 163 hours or, as Schor put it, "the equivalent of an extra month a year."[51] Workers worked both longer weeks (about one hour longer) and more weeks per year (about three weeks more).[52] (For the sake of comparison, a worker who works 40 hours a week for a whole year, less two weeks' vacation time and another two weeks' worth of individual holidays, will put in about 1,920 hours.) This increase, Schor continued, had not been offset by employees doing less work in the household. Men on average were doing more than they used to, and women less than before (but still more than men); but when all was averaged out, full-time employees in 1987 still did 888 hours per year of household work, virtually the same as in 1969.[53]

But the United States is a rich country with a generally growing economy. Why, asked Schor, do we work more and consume more, rather than harvesting economic growth as increased leisure? Capitalist institutions, she answered, have an inherent tendency toward long working hours. This tendency was dampened in the early part of this century by a combination of trade union pressure and public action, but since the Second World War these countervailing forces have slackened, and the natural tendency has indeed been augmented by intense international competition. Employers, Schor contended, prefer higher-paid, longer-worked employees because such intense jobs allow them to have fewer, more qualified workers; because long-working employees are more dependent on their jobs and therefore easier to control; and because companies need to provide only one set of fringe benefits for each worker, regardless of how long he or she works.[54] Having to pay time-and-a-half for overtime, although a burden, is simply not a sufficient counterweight to these other forces. Moreover, said Schor, once workers are making the higher wages, they become accustomed to them and they, too, do not want to trade fewer work hours for a cut in pay.

Shortly thereafter, a very different story, covering virtually the same time span, was told by John P. Robinson and Geoffrey Godbey in a book entitled *Time for Life*.[55] Robinson and Godbey reported hours of paid work for employed men declining from 46.5 hours per week in 1965 to 42.9 in 1975, and further to 39.7 in 1985. For employed women, a similar trend showed reductions from 36.8 hours per week in 1965 to 30.8 in 1985; however, since female participation in the paid labor force grew over those two decades, the average number of paid hours for women as a whole increased from 17.5 hours per week to 20.3 hours per week.[56] During the same time period, the number of hours spent on housework by women, employed or not employed, fell a good bit, while those spent by men, employed or not employed, grew; the time parents spent on child care was more constant.[57] The upshot was that what Robinson and Godbey called "Trends in Total Productive Activity" (paid work and time spent commuting to work, plus housework, child care, and necessary shopping) showed for women a considerable reduction from 59.4 hours a week in 1965 to 52.3 in 1975, with a slight bounce back to 53.2 in 1985; for men, there was a substantial reduction from 59.1 hours per week in 1965 to 53.7 in 1975, and this fell slightly further to 53.1 in 1985.[58] Or, to rephrase the point in terms of available free time (time that is neither productive nor devoted to personal care like sleeping and dressing), according to Robinson and Godbey there was a 5-hour-per-week increase in free time after 1965, with most of the gain occurring between 1965 and 1975. This, they said—in near-direct opposition to Schor's claim—"translates to a gain of more than six 40-hour workweeks of additional free time per year, or an additional month and a half of vacation."[59] (What are people doing with this additional free time? According to Robinson and Godbey, what they are mostly doing is watching TV.)[60]

The Overworked American or *Time for Life:* these are quite different accounts of our situation. Not surprisingly, they are based on quite different methods for gathering information. Schor began with data collected by means of the government's asking large numbers of people to estimate how many hours they worked in the prior week; Robinson and Godbey started with a smaller number of individual time diaries, kept contemporaneously, minute-by-minute, for a single day. Although the results of the studies are very different, neither method seems obviously flawed, and it is doubtful that the differences between the two positions can be fully resolved. There is no third measure of unquestioned accuracy against which to judge the two contending methods.[61]

Partly as a result of these works—the Schor book in particular was a best-seller—the headlines have in recent years been full of claims that Americans do (or do not) work too long. But whoever is right as to the movement of the overall averages, how we evaluate the situation may depend on what we understand the underlying dynamics to be.

By Schor's account, a large part—more than two-thirds—of the increase in working hours that she reported came from people working more weeks per year rather than more hours per week.[62] A large part of this weeks-worked increase was, in turn, the result of women's weeks worked coming closer to what men's had already been.[63] In short, the "extra month a year" that she announced was heavily influenced by the large increase in weeks worked on average by working women, from 39.3 weeks per year to 45.4. That figure, still below the 48.5 weeks per year typical of working men, might be seen as a sign of social equalization rather than any relentless dynamic of capitalist oppression. It is not so clear that there is an evil here waiting to be addressed.

Moreover, the widespread publicity that has recently attended this issue must be understood partly in life-cycle terms—or, rather, in terms of the life-cycle as lived by the baby boomers, who, because of the size of their age cohort, have been particularly well covered by the media. The age-graded data are striking. According to Robinson and Godbey, people aged 18–24 and 55–64 have as much as 10 to 12 hours a week more free time than do the age cohorts in between. This differential is larger than the increase which, on the authors' calculations, had occurred in the amount of free time available at any particular age. As a result, people who were 18 years old in 1965—the leading edge of the baby boomers—and who were thus 38 in 1985, experienced over those twenty years a reduction, on average, of about 5 hours a week in their free time, even on the optimistic account of Robinson and Godbey showing that they enjoyed more free time in their late thirties than their parents had enjoyed at the same age.[64] But it is no real surprise—and nothing new—that people who have the responsibilities of being married and having young children, and working besides, have the least free time.

Overall, then, it seems fair to say that there is no general social crisis in the amount of time Americans as a whole work, either in the narrow sense of paid work or in the broader sense of doing necessary tasks. Even if we accept the worse-case analysis—and it is not clear that it is the truer one—we are working only a bit more (especially on a weekly basis) than we worked a generation ago, which is still much less than we worked for several generations before that.

Both of these books are based on data from the middle 1980s. It might be thought that the substantial changes since then in the economy, and in how businesses are run, have revolutionized working hours as well. This does not, however, seem to be true as a general matter. In an update to their work using data (albeit not wholly comparable data) through 1995, Robinson and Godbey reported that while it was true that both men and women worked a bit more in 1995 than they had in 1985, the figure was still considerably below that for 1965.[65] The Census Bureau's statistics show, for the 1990s, a rather small gain in the number of hours that employees work, and a rather larger decline in the number of hours worked by the self-employed.[66]

What instead seems to be the case is that changes in the economy have affected the distribution of hours among jobs much more than they have moved the overall averages. In recent years there has been a growth (or, historically speaking, a reemergence) of jobs with very long hours—jobs more than 25 percent longer than the 40-hour standard, jobs that cannot be seen as the 40-hour week plus a few hours of occasional overtime. Of men in their middle years (aged 25–54) in non-agricultural employment, 22.2 percent worked 49 or more hours per week in 1976; by 1993, 29.2 percent did. The comparable figures for women are 5.7 percent and 12.0 percent.[67] Much of this increase happened in the late 1980s. In 1985, almost 17 million non-agricultural employees, men and women, worked 49 hours or more per week; by 1993 the figure had jumped to almost 22 million.[68]

How has this happened with the FLSA in place? There are three possibilities: the law has been flouted; the overtime "premium" is not an adequate deterrent to employers' requiring overtime; or the growth has occurred in occupations exempt from the Act's overtime provisions.

Because of its wide scope and the diversity of situations to which it applies, the FLSA is a law that is hard to enforce. But the typical case of flouting the law occurs at the bottom of the economic scale, where workers are too poor and too unskilled (and perhaps too illegally in the United States) to complain effectively; and where employers stand to gain not only by not paying the overtime premium, but by not paying the minimum wage as well. This type of overtime work may well escape the statisticians just as it does the enforcers. In any case, it does not explain the statistics just recited. For insofar as the statisticians can record the phenomenon, there is a strong positive correlation between weekly earnings and very long hours. Indeed, in 1995, of those who earned the very high sum of over $2000 a week, more than 60 percent worked 49 hours per week or more.[69] If this pattern were the result of flouting the law, it would indicate that employers try to escape from the law more, and employees and the government try to enforce the law less, as employees get richer. While this proposition has a certain Robin Hood appeal, as an empirical claim it seems highly doubtful.

The second possibility—that time-and-a-half does not have the same deterrent effect on long hours that it once had—is probably true. Employers' calculations have changed since the FLSA was passed because of the growth of fringe benefits; these are, historically, creatures of World War II and the postwar period.[70] Insofar as these benefits, such as health insurance, have become substantial and do not vary by the number of hours worked—this is an employer-by-employer question—it may be cheaper to pay existing employees premium wages for overtime hours than to incur the cost of the new batch of benefits attendant on hiring a new worker. At the least, the differential may be considerably less than "time-and-a-half" suggests.[71]

That an increased willingness by employers to pay overtime premiums even for very long hours is a factor here is suggested by the fact that there has been some increase in jobs with very long hours in every employment category.[72] Thus, if we want to maintain the 40-hour norm, there is a case to be made either for raising the overtime premium, or for including fringe benefits in the base rate on which the premium is calculated. But the failure of time-and-a-half to create a sufficient disincentive does not seem to be the whole story. For the job categories in which very-long-hour jobs cluster most, are also those categories to which the overtime requirements, in whole or in part, simply do not apply.[73]

This brings us to the third possibility: that very long hours exist in large part because of exemptions from the FLSA; indeed, that they exist mostly because of one particular exemption. As of 1996, the Department of Labor estimated that somewhat over 31.5 million employees were exempt from the 40-hour work week because they were employees (in the language of the Act) "employed in a bona fide executive, administrative, or professional capacity";[74] this group constituted almost two-thirds of all those exempt for any reason whatsoever.[75] 31.5 million employees is a very large number, and indeed represents just over a quarter of the total of more than 122 million wage and salary employees (that is, not including the self-employed) in the United States. Many members of this group work very long hours, and in many cases longer hours than they used to. Between 1985 and 1993, according to another set of government data, the proportion of managers working 49 hours or more per week increased from about 40 percent to about 45 percent; for professional employees, the percentage rose from the low 30s to the high 30s.[76]

Why does the FLSA exclude executive, administrative, and professional employees? An exception for upper-level employees appeared in the Act from the earliest drafts, carrying over experience from the NIRA Codes. Was the exclusion made because executive, administrative, and professional personnel were thought to have ample bargaining power, and not to be in need of the law's added protection? Was it because they were assumed not to be paid on an hourly basis, and thus the law's technical provisions would not easily fit their situation? Was it because they were assumed to work widely fluctuating hours to which the concepts of "time" and "overtime" did not apply? Was it because of an image of the "executive" as someone indispensable, someone whose tasks could not be delegated just because "time" was up? Or was it merely an adoption into law of status distinctions drawn from the larger society? The matter was simply not debated.[77]

In any case, we need to evaluate this exemption in light of our reconstructed understanding of the FLSA—in light, that is, of a purpose to provide a proper balance of time for work and for other socially important activities. The fact that executive, administrative, and professional employees are, generally speaking, well paid—that we do not have to worry about avoiding oppression in any obvious sense—does not speak to this concern. But this is not always understood. For example, when in 1996 Congress decided to address specially the new class of workers it described as "computer systems analyst, computer programmer, software engineer, or other similarly skilled worker," it provided that they would be exempt from the 40-hour week if they were "compensated at a rate of not less than $27.63 an hour."[78] This certainly ensured that no one who lost premium pay was getting a low wage. But it did little to control the long hours of a group of workers almost proverbial for working them.[79]

If balance is our goal, we have to conclude that the ordinary workings of the marketplace in the absence of legal controls are not producing the desired result—for the many executives, administrators, and professionals who are working very long hours, and for society. Like others, many members of this group are now part of two-career families and have to make a different accommodation to family responsibilities than that typical of earlier generations. Executives and professionals also traditionally have played a large role in civic groups; when they work very long hours, they are less able to provide their skills in this socially valuable way. These problems of working too long are exacerbated by the increasing sense of formlessness of work among professionals and managers: they are always on call, never secure in the knowledge that work has stopped. Formlessness at work means that the alternative rhythms of not-work time have more difficulty establishing themselves. Even in the United States, which values work very highly, and even for these employees, who have in many respects the best jobs there are, work is meant to have limits.

Indeed, from one point of view the situation of this group of employees is worse than for most lower-ranking workers. Managers—and increasingly professionals—are typically salaried. Not only do longer hours not cost their employers time-and-a-half; they cost nothing additional at all. There is no disincentive to stop employers from demanding long—and, if one's goal is a balanced life, excessive—hours.[80] (Perhaps not surprisingly, a recent survey showed that high levels of feeling overworked correlated strongly both with working more than 50 hours a week and with feeling pressured by employers to work those hours rather than choosing them for personal reasons.)[81]

It may seem unrealistic to expect people like these to work only 40 hours in a standard work week—but why is that so? The image of the professional or executive as completely in charge of his or her own time, true or not for the 1930s, hardly fits most of the class today. They are increasingly subjected to the same sort of organizational forms and institutional constraints that other workers have long faced. Lawyers, for instance, were only beginning to charge by the hour in the 1930s;[82] now many of them keep track of their billing time in units as small as a tenth of an hour. Young lawyers in large firms are expected to turn in a specified number of "billable hours" each year or face the consequences. (Professional time, the sociologists would say, has been "commodified.") Furthermore, a good part of the present situation developed out of a conscious effort to re-engineer organizations to reduce the number of white-collar employees—the "downsizing" of the late 1980s. Now the mania for managers and professionals always to be at work, or at least to be in direct contact with work, grows on itself; it is expected because it happens and happens because it is expected. This is not something "inherent in the situation"; but it is also not something that individuals can easily change by themselves. They face job competition from those who are willing to work the 50 or 60 hours demanded; and they face a set of external (and often internalized) social norms which make working "only" 40 hours seem like slacking off. At the same time, while many high-level employees think of long hours as necessary, that does not mean that they think of them as desirable or right. In these sorts of circumstances, control of hours worked (as both trade unions and legislators have long known) requires collective action.

It would be very desirable for there to be social norms that set a limit and a form to the ordinary hours of work for executive, administrative, and professional employees. It is, however, not so easy to fashion the rule that is needed. As a practical matter, it is hard to subject to a time limit much of the work done by these high-level employees. They do not punch time clocks; many do not keep track of their time for business purposes; and much of their work is not done at a specific business location. Nor is it necessarily easy to give their work form. Their job demands are often unpredictable—and, for those who deal in an international arena, they are often subject to the outside influence of an entirely different set of social clocks. Some people—although probably fewer than those who think so—are truly indispensable, hour by hour, to the operation of their businesses or organizations. Finally, the coerciveness of any such new norm would be felt not only by employers, but also by many employees—either because they do work that they find enjoyable even when done for long hours, or because they have internalized long-work-time mores.

A sensible solution might be to split the group of workers "employed in a bona fide executive, administrative, or professional capacity" into smaller groups with different characteristics. Some parts of this group work in situations where they either have regular hours or already keep track of their hours for business purposes. For these workers, it would make sense simply to abolish the exemption: this is straightforward; it builds on the 40-hour norm present in the society as a whole even if not actualized in many of these subgroups; and it eliminates a "class" distinction in the law that no longer corresponds to organizational realities. This may seem "unthinkable," but only until it is actually "thought"; for example, lawyers for the federal government (and many other government personnel who would otherwise be "exempt" under the FLSA) are subject to a separate statutory scheme which sets 40 hours as the basic work week and provides for overtime pay or other compensation.[83] If they are so treated, why not others? Doubtless there would have to be a transitional period in which salaries would be readjusted to this form of remuneration and in which the dividing line between "time" and "overtime" would be slowly reduced to 40 from a starting figure perhaps as high as 48 hours per week. But in the end we would have an acceptable standard for professionals and executives, which, like the existing standard for most employees, sets a norm that is flexible, but only at a price. (The point of exacting that price for employees like these is, of course, not to put more money in their pockets but rather to give their employers an incentive to rearrange the demands of work.) Setting that standard would not only be of direct value to the employees involved; it would also help reinforce the norm the FLSA embodies as a basic part of the culture, since many of these workers are, in some sense, setters of trends.

This would still leave a group of high-level employees who work disparate and irregular hours without any ordinary reason to keep track of them. They could be simply left as exempt workers. But even for this group, some progress toward establishing a norm of work time might be made by thinking not in terms of hours per week, but rather in terms of the structure of the time spent at work. For, as we shall shortly see, it might be possible to protect directly some form of communal not-at-work time.

The argument presented thus far in favor of the 40-hour week comes to this: There is no natural limit to work considered by itself. But it is important that there be some limit to work because of the many other significant activities that people engage in. The convention of our society, stable since its enactment into the FLSA in the late 1930s, is that the 40-hour work week is the norm.

Despite the many social and economic changes since it was established, this standard has worked pretty well; there is no general crisis of work time. The most significant problem that has arisen is the relatively recent growth in particular categories of jobs requiring very long hours; this problem might well be addressed by creative enlargement of the applicable scope of the FLSA.

This argument, it might be said, is fine as far as it goes. But one might also say that its emphasis on individuals' working time and on society-wide averages misses what many would consider to be the real point: the way in which work time interacts with the new organization of the American family.

The question might be put this way: does the FLSA's construction of the 40-hour work week in effect assume a man-at-the-workplace, woman-at-home pattern? Certainly at the time the Act was passed, and for innumerable years before, the general social pattern was that women worked when they were young and single, but stopped working either when they got married or when they had their first child.[84] Even in 1950, after the Second World War, only 12.6 percent of married mothers with children under 17 were in the labor force; in 1994, however, 69 percent were.[85] Not only are more women working now, but they are also working more. Especially important is the growth in the number of women in their middle years who work as full-time, year-round employees. As late as 1976, fewer than half of working women aged 25 to 54 worked this way; by the early 1990s, just over 60 percent did.[86] Any discussion of how patterns of work fit with patterns of family life (and of religious and civic life as well) must take this new reality into account.

The demands placed on families by these new working patterns are the subject of another recent book, Arlie R. Hochschild's *The Time Bind*.[87] To investigate the matter, Hochschild studied the employees, top to bottom, of a large company that was known for being "family friendly." What she saw was that although workers

said they were time-stressed, they made almost no use of programs that would allow them to cut back on the amount of time
they worked. Virtually no one voluntarily worked part-time or
shared a job. This was not merely a question of financial need:
workers did not even take all of the paid vacation time they had
coming to them gratis. The only popular program was "flextime," which allowed workers to rearrange their hours but did
not reduce the time worked.[88] Yet the opportunities workers did
not use were, Hochschild concluded, sincerely offered by the
company, and were not just for "show."[89]

What Hochschild found was that a combination of cultural
and social forces were leading working parents in some sense to
decide to work as hard as they did. These forces impinged differently on different workers, but they included the following: the
belief that working long hours is a sign of ambition, and will lead
to advancement; the belief that working overtime fulfills one's
role as a provider; the belief that women have to work as long as
men do in order to get respect, and in order to support claims for
equal participation by men in house and family work; the fact
that friends and relationships are made at work, and, especially
among those working unusual shifts, may be the main sources of
social support; the fact that it is often easier to do a recognizably
"good job" at work than with the more diffuse tasks of the home
and family; and the fact that family life is often simply less emo-
tionally "safe" than life at work. Hochschild concluded that these
attachments to work, although in some respects perhaps good in
themselves, were leading parents to overemphasize work at the
cost of home and family. Children, she said, were being forced
into "tight-fitting temporal uniforms" in order to meet the demands of an overly scheduled day.[90]

Stated more broadly, the real danger with work time may well
lie not specifically in the number of hours allocated to it, but in
the way it tends to set a structure which heavily influences the

possibilities for coordination and rhythm regarding all other social connections. Even if the number of minutes spent working is
exactly the same, there is, for example, a large difference between
someone's working at home on household tasks, which can often
be interspersed with family and even civic time, and someone's
going to work at a workplace separated from these other connections. In the first situation, activities that directly support family
life can establish a rhythm of their own, and the time spent on
other productive tasks can be rescheduled in order to make the
coordination of social life possible; in the second, the highly organized scheduling and rhythm of the workplace threatens to
make other scheduling, and other rhythms, impossible.

The danger of yielding our structure of time to work's demands is clearly much greater when such a large part of the population, and all of the adults in so many families, work full-time.
But the problem is not easy to address because, as Hochschild's
work illustrates, so many important social connections are now
made through work itself. The workplace has become, especially
in the last thirty or forty years, a major place—perhaps *the* major
place—for making contact with others in circumstances that generate a feeling of belonging to a group. And on the individual
level, work has become identity; asking and answering "what do
you do?" is now a basic way in which people come to know each
other. In these circumstances, the most desirable length for work
time is not necessarily the fewest hours that will generate an adequate income; nor can the workplace rhythm be viewed as merely
of interest to employers, since it has such meaning for workers.
The question, instead, is again one of balance: giving work time,
in all its facets, its due, but also keeping it, in all its facets, within
bounds.

Does the 40-hour week, in the context of dual-fulltime-working
(or single-fulltime-working) parents, strike this balance, or is the
number too high? This is partly an intricate issue of counting and

scheduling hours. For example, it has been suggested that if the work week were reduced to 32 hours, it would then be possible to give dual-earner families the choice of caring for their own children, by working at offsetting hours.[91] But one may well question whether the overall rhythm involved in having all child care provided by two working spouses, even if they are working only 32 hours each, is desirable. For this is a rhythm in which children see a great deal of their parents one at a time, but the parents see each other very little, and the whole family, as a temporal entity, barely exists. Parents who try to do this within the current work week find it very stressful; divorce rates among couples working different shifts are very high.[92] And if less work means less pay, then this restructuring might eliminate the alternative choice of both spouses working synchronously and making enough money to pay for quality child care.[93]

But much of the issue is less directly practical and more a question of what the culture views as appropriate and meaningful. In light of the positive value of work and of relationships at the workplace, it is important for work to have a certain "bulk" or "substantiality"; for many people, like many of Hochschild's informants, it is important that they have a "full-time" job. Through a historical process, the cultural norm for what constitutes a full-time job has been set at 40 hours. Since history goes on, it is certainly possible that the standard will at some point be reset downward. Individuals and employers might, over time, increasingly arrange for work that is, by present standards, "part-time." For the moment, the 40-hour week has the enormous power of the norm that "is."

This analysis suggest two conclusions. First, the case for legally mandating a shorter work week has not been made. Second, if we are to attend to the needs of modern families, and of other important social institutions, we have to consider not simply the number of hours worked, but also the ways in which the work week is structured. The very significance of work in modern life—the importance that helps justify the 40-hour week even if both parents are working it—requires us to focus on setting the boundaries of work time so that other social activities can be co-ordinated and other rhythms created. Partly this is a matter of defining who gets to control the boundary lines between work time and "off" time, when there is a dispute: that is the topic of Chapter 6. But partly it is a question of whether "40 hours a week," even if it is a proper allocation of time to work, represents an adequate consideration of the other facets of time: coordination, rhythm, and texture.

There are, in the abstract, a great many ways to locate 40 hours of work within the week that contains 168 hours spread over seven days and nights. It is of great importance, however, whether all of these possibilities are equally used, or whether, instead, work time exhibits a pattern. It might seem, from a first glance at productive efficiency, that the uniform dispersal of work over all the hours of the week has a certain appeal: it would allow not only for the continuous employment of expensive machinery, but also for the more even, and therefore more efficient, use of the many necessary supports for production, ranging from the generation of electric power to the movement of commuters on the highways. Even from the point of view of the work experience itself, however, this analysis is insufficient. As we saw in the previous chapter, it seems that workplaces often do not work well even at a technical level if people are not brought together to co-ordinate work activities; and social connections such as those Arlie Hochschild discovered (which of course have implications for long-term productivity as well as personal satisfaction) depend on individuals' being together at work at the same time.

However, because the tendency in our society is for work time to dominate other activities, its structure is of special importance in regard to family time, religious time, civic time, and social time.

Raising a family, going to church, participating in public meetings, attending a concert—these are all social activities. They require expanses of time when groups of people are together free
from work. If activities like these are to establish their own
rhythms, they require that work time not only be limited, but
limited in recurrent, stable patterns. The issue is not so much the
shape of work time, but rather the shape of its reflexive image,
not-work time. If work time lacks a social pattern—if all hours
and days are, from the point of view of society, like all others; if
people go to work and come home from work equally at all hours
of the week—individuals will still work and not-work. But neither at work, nor especially when participating in the socially
vital activities that constitute not-working, will they be able to
coordinate easily with others and establish the rhythms and textures of time needed for a balanced set of social commitments.

In light of the history we have already reviewed, it seems clear
that the assumption of those who enacted the Fair Labor Standards Act was that the "40-hour week" generally meant "five 8-
hour days." Moreover, those days were probably thought to be
Monday through Friday—certainly not Sunday, given the vi-
brancy of the Blue Laws at that time. As to the hours of the day,
daytime work was surely the most common.

At the same time, those who wrote the FLSA could not have
assumed temporal uniformity throughout the economy. Even
without considering agricultural labor (which was excluded from
the Act), then as now there were numerous other occupations
that either required continuous attention (such as work at industrial plants that had to be kept open around the clock because it
was too expensive to shut them down) or that were specifically
countercyclical (such as being a minister). In any case, the Act
mandates that work be organized with reference to the week—
the 40-hour limit is required to be counted on a weekly basis,
rather than averaged over a longer period of time—but it says

nothing about how work time is to be organized with reference to the days of the week or the hours of the day.

Today, the popular image of the "standard work week" of course distributes the 40 hours as 9:00 to 5:00, Monday to Friday. But what is the reality? How many Americans in fact work according to that schedule, and how many work at different times? Labor market analysts, using data collected now and again by the government's Bureau of Labor Statistics, have tried to create a composite analysis of a highly variegated economy; while some details are in dispute, the broad picture is fairly clear.[94]

Let us start with the question of what hours in the day people work. The image may be 9:00 to 5:00, but in fact there is considerable variation in the precise hour when people go to work: a considerable number start between 6:30 and 7:30 A.M.; more between 7:30 and 8:30; and somewhat fewer between 8:30 and 9:30. There are similar variations in returning home in the late afternoon.[95] If we view the matter somewhat more broadly, however—if we ask who works a regular daytime schedule any time between 6:00 A.M. and 6:00 P.M., as contrasted with an evening shift, a night shift, a rotating shift, a split shift, or simply an irregular schedule—then we find considerable regularity: over four-fifths of full-time workers work a regular day shift.[96] (There are, of course, a few occupations in which alternative shifts are much more common, such as food-service workers, or policemen and firemen.)[97] Since these day shifts, whenever they start, are long enough to overlap, there are correspondingly several hours in the later morning and early afternoon when more than 80 percent of workers are on the job at the same time. By contrast, starting in the late evening and continuing through the wee hours, fewer (often considerably fewer) than 10 percent are working.[98]

These data change somewhat, but not startlingly so, if we focus specifically on the work patterns of dual-career couples. If we divide the work day into the broad categories of day, evening, and night work, husbands and wives without children are very likely—more than just randomly likely—to be at work, and not at work, at the same times. This correlation decreases when the couples have children, especially very young children; mothers of small children, although they work for pay less than women in general do, disproportionately work in the evening or at night.[99] There is, in other words, some prevalence of split-shift parenting for the very young. Because most work is daytime work, however, the most common pattern even among married couples with toddlers in the house is for both parents to work daytime shifts.[100]

Turning to the question of days of the week: do most American workers really work Monday through Friday? Again putting farm workers to one side, about three-quarters of employees work a five-day work week; if we speak only of full-time employees, over four-fifths do.[101] However, the five days worked are not necessarily Monday through Friday. Indeed, if one takes together those who work only five days but including at least one of the weekend days, and those whose work hours are spread over more than five days in the week, there are a considerable number of people doing weekend work. (The figure is even larger if one includes self-employed people, who are not subject to the FLSA; for although the self-employed are a small fraction of the work force, they are much more likely to work six or seven days per week.)[102] Estimates vary, but one recent study based on 1997 data found that only 7 out of 10 full-time employees worked weekdays only; 3 out of 10 did some weekend work.[103] Saturday work is, of course, much more common than Sunday work.[104]

Clearly, there is sufficient variation in these figures that it is a mistake to translate "the 40-hour week" into "the 9:00 to 5:00 Monday through Friday week"; many people work different hours. At the same time, it is also clear that there is a social pattern to working time; work hours are not in any sense dispersed evenly over the possible hours in the week. If instead of 9:00 to

5:00 we speak of daytime shifts, and if instead of Monday through Friday we speak of Monday through Saturday (but not necessarily including all the days in between), then we have described a pattern that includes a very large part of the working population.

Should this pattern be accepted as "normal" or rejected as "deviant"? Does it simply represent inevitable variation in the rhythms of work, or is it a frayed pattern in need of mending?

Actual working hours, it seems, are much less compact than our stereotype of them would lead us to believe. Consequently, even within a framework of allocating 40 hours per worker per week, the available amount of socially coordinated not-work time is smaller than we might have imagined. Whether we think this leaves time to coordinate the many other valuable activities of life, and to give them the rhythm and meaning they deserve, depends in large part on what activities we have in mind. For activities which occur in the evenings and on weekends, and which do not depend on the presence of a precisely identified group of people—for spectator sports, most religious services, and many civic meetings, for example—this pattern seems adequate. Certainly it is a long way from the undifferentiated time world of 24/7, or of the Soviet "continuous production week" discussed in the last chapter. Most people can come to such activities. By contrast, for activities which happen during the weekday or early evening, and which do depend on the presence of specific people—for many after-work sports teams, various social clubs, and, above all, many family activities (like family meals)—the fuzziness of the pattern presents much greater problems. The increased prevalence of dual-career families makes these problems more apparent, for two workers can both have their schedules fall within the general pattern and still differ substantially in the structure of their non-work time. But even for a single worker, the problem of coordinating with others can look very different depending on where the individual is located within the general social pattern of work time.

It thus seems that the workers at the company studied by Hochschild had a good understanding of the dynamics of their situations when they considered flexibility of work time the most important "family-friendly" benefit they could have. Indeed, workers in general have, in recent years, shown considerable interest in increasing the flexibility of their working hours. Partly, no doubt, this simply reflects a desire for personal freedom and control, but surely more important is a hope that with increased flexibility, the responsibilities of two-job dual parents (or one-job single parents) will become more manageable. What workers are looking for is not the ability to situate their work anywhere within the imaginable 168 hours of the week, for if people worked at widely varying hours no coordination would be possible. Rather, they want to be able to refine the general social pattern of work we have been looking at to allow for the needed coordination of the non-work activities of the particular people involved.

Two of the ways—probably the two most commonly mentioned ways—for achieving increased work-time flexibility within the ordinary work week are fully compatible with the FLSA's stipulation of a 40-hour week. "Flextime" in its most common form—in which the employee has flexibility concerning when to arrive at work, when to have lunch, when to leave, so long as certain "core" hours are covered and the normal number of hours of daily work are rendered—presents no problem because the total number of hours worked per day and per week does not change. The second option, the compressed work week, generally assumes the form of a 10-hour, four-day work week. This also fits within the FLSA strictures because it changes only the number of hours worked per day, and not the number per week that is relevant to the statute.

The four-day, 10-hours-per-day work week would, however, fall afoul of a statute which stipulated not only that the standard work week should contain not more than 40 hours, but also that the standard work day should contain not more than 8; overtime would have to be paid for the ninth and tenth hour each day. In fact, there is a considerable history of such statutes. Even before the Fair Labor Standards Act was passed, the laws that governed work on U.S. government contracts stipulated the 8-hour day as well as the 40-hour week. Well after the Act was passed, many states had labor laws stipulating overtime after 8 hours per day within their own jurisdictions. But almost all such legislation has now been abolished, with much of the change coming in the 1980s and 1990s.[105] As of the turn of the millennium, only Alaska, Nevada, and California retained 8-hour-day laws, and in California, the laws had seesawed back and forth on this issue over the preceding decade.[106]

Whether these legal changes had much to do with the trend or not—the statistics do not distinguish among the various forms of flexible work time—the growth in flexibility at work is one of the few clear changes in the social organization of work time to have occurred over the last two decades. According to Bureau of Labor Statistics figures, the proportion of workers with some degree of flexibility in their hours, while still well short of a majority, increased from 12.4 percent in 1985 to 27.6 percent in 1997.[107] The only serious problem with expanding the flexibility of work time would be if it began to be used to stretch the basic social pattern beyond even its present fuzzy contours—if its use, that is, led to an expansion in evening, night, and weekend (especially Sunday) work. Given what most workers want flexibility for—to adjust their schedules to coordinate with others—it seems doubtful that they would go in this direction. Of course, from the point of view of the structure of not-work time, it is of considerable importance to know whether it is the employer or the employee who gets to control the "flex" in flextime; we will return to this issue in Chapter 6.

This analysis still leaves us with the question of where the society is heading next. Is the pattern of working hours that we have looked at a stable one? Or are we witnessing the beginning of a slide to a world in which work time is much more dispersed than it now is? Is it true, as one demographer recently wrote, that "the '9-to-5' workday does not appear to be in jeopardy of fading from its prominence in U.S. workplaces"?[108] Or is it rather the case, as another demographer claims, that "Americans are moving toward a 24-hour, 7-day-a-week economy"?[109]

Unfortunately, we do not know. Partly the problem is lack of consistent data collected over a long enough period of time to reveal trends reliably. Until relatively recently, data collection focused on the simple question of how many hours were worked per week, without much thought given to how those work hours were distributed within the week.[110] The best figures that we have are government data collected in 1985, 1991, and 1997 which seem to show little variation over those twelve years in the proportion of workers working alternative shifts;[111] we have no comparable set of data for weekend work. But a larger part of the problem in determining where we are heading is that any overall change in the pattern of work will be a cumulation of many smaller changes, and there is no reason to think these are all going in the same direction. Working alternative shifts is especially common in restaurant work and in health care; with more people going out to eat, and an aging population, we can expect these sectors of the economy to grow. But many highly capitalized industries typical of the "old" economy also frequently have unusual work shifts, and they probably will not grow. In addition, the impact of new technologies is uncertain. The speeded-up expectations engendered by e-mail and the Internet—the sense that the economy is always "on call"—might lead to more work being done overnight or on weekends; however, technology can also be used to "time-shift" so that orders are placed at night but filled during the day, and international data communication can result in the processing work going overseas to be done "overnight" in the daylight hours of other time zones.

In short, insofar as the matter of working hours turns on the rise or fall in importance of, or the work patterns common in, various sectors of the economy, it is a complex topic and one that cannot be settled except by collecting standardized data over a longer period of time than we have so far. The most that can be concluded from the published studies, based on data collected from 1985 onward, is a couple of tentative propositions. First, if there has been any movement in the last decade and a half, it has been toward a greater dispersion of work patterns. Second, whatever movement has occurred has been more toward an increase in weekend work than toward an increase in night work.

Thus, whether the Fair Labor Standards Act is adequate for its job—whether it provides a sufficient structure for work time—is in important respects still debatable. Work hours seem to retain a weekly rhythm, and especially with the demise of the Blue Laws, the FLSA's insistence that work not only be limited, but be limited by the week, seems an important support for this fundamental social practice. If we can assume within the week the more particular pattern of work we have investigated, then the flexibility allowed by the FLSA seems productive, since it provides room for the finer adjustments needed by families and other small social groups. However, the underspecificity of the FLSA vis-à-vis this pattern also leaves room for a deleterious increase in the formlessness of work time. Thus we face the possibility that without further legal support, the dispersion of private workplace arrangements could well be so great that not-work time would be insufficiently social.

Whether the times call for further measures is, given the empirical uncertainties, obviously a matter of judgment. But it is at least worth thinking about what could be done if and when there is the political will to do something. It is not uncommon in collective bargaining agreements to stipulate that any Saturday work, even if otherwise within the 40-hour week, be paid at the time-and-a-half rate, and that any Sunday work be paid double-time.[112] These provisions establish a gradient of incentives which help protect the weekend even as they permit the flexibility to do any work that is very valuable if done at that time. Provisions like these could be written into the law,[113] and similar ones could be established to protect evening and nighttime hours as well. Such measures may strike some as illiberal, as foolishly preventing people from doing what they want to do. But they can also be seen as enabling measures that make possible the carrying out of various valuable not-work activities in a society in which work is so very important—especially those activities that require the coordination of considerable numbers of people.[114]

Indeed, laws like these might be used to maintain a pattern of work even for those otherwise exempted from the 40-hour-week rule. For example, if it proves difficult to include within the 40-hour week some of those in the "executive, administrative, or professional" class now exempted from the FLSA, it may still be possible to include them in the general proposition that, insofar as they work, say, overnight, or on Sundays, their employers must be prepared to pay a premium. This would clearly not be the equivalent of requiring the 40-hour-maximum week, but if it is hard to set a limit to the allocation of time to certain jobs, establishing a recurrent form for them would still help control the rhythm of work, and thereby help the other rhythms of life survive.

The 40-hour work week, as we have seen, is more than a mere allocation of time. It sets a social pattern as well, partly by the force of law (which makes the week a mandatory boundary) and partly by the force of custom (which for most people arranges the 40 hours in one of only a few of the many conceivable ways of arranging them). This structure of work time is immensely important to the maintenance of other social possibilities that might otherwise be crowded out by the demands of work. It is hard to know at the present time how stable the structure is. If the FLSA proves to be inadequate to maintaining the structure of work time, it will be important to take additional steps.

It is not only the FLSA that supports this structure, however; other bodies of law do, too. One of the chief counterforces to the dispersion of work time, the legal maintenance of Sunday and of holidays, has, as we have seen, become very attenuated. But there is still one very powerful external countervailing force to the homogenization of work time, and that is the structure of school time. That school time has a great impact on work time is perhaps easy to overlook, since one assumes that virtually every child who goes to school works little if at all. But children are a large part of the society, and how they live helps set its tone. Moreover, from a purely practical point of view, a great many workers have to make adjustments to coordinate with school time because they have children in school; and a great many employers have to let workers make these adjustments because going to school is the social and legal norm. To see the whole picture, then, we must investigate school time: what is its structure, and how does it relate to the structure of work?

5

SCHOOL TIME

In 1991, the United States Congress established a high-level study group, The National Education Commission on Time and Learning, and directed it to investigate "the quality and adequacy of the study and learning time of elementary and secondary students in the United States."[1] The Commission reported that schools throughout the United States follow a very distinctive time pattern. The norm for required attendance is 180 school days. With allowance for weekends and holidays, these 180 days stretch across a school year which, with few exceptions, begins in late summer (late August or early September) and closes near the end of spring (usually in June). On each day, schools usually open and close at fixed times from the morning to the early afternoon: "a school in one district," said the Commission, "might open at 7:30 A.M. and close at 2:15 P.M.; in another, the school day might run from 8:00 in the morning until 3:00 in the afternoon." Within that day, there is, on average, 5.6 hours of classroom time, although much of that time may be spent on courses and activities other than core academic subjects.[2]

"Unyielding and relentless," the Commission said, "the time available in a uniform six-hour day and a 180-day year is the unacknowledged design flaw in American education."[3] Schools should be reinvented with an eye to the varying learning styles and needs of different kinds of pupils, which would entail much more flexible uses of time; as things stood, schools were (in the title of the Commission's report) "Prisoners of Time."

Was the Commission correct in its view that the current organization of time devoted to schooling is dysfunctional from an educational point of view? We shall look at that question in a moment. But first we should notice that the Commission was certainly right in treating school time as a social pattern with considerable force. From a more general point of view, schools (or our system of schooling) could as well be described, not as "prisoners," but rather as "shapers" of time.

According to the recent census, 281.4 million people lived in the United States in 2000;[4] of these, 48.7 million were enrolled in an elementary or secondary school.[5] Most of this large part of the population—somewhere between one out of every six Americans and one out of every five—lives by a rhythm dictated to them by a double feature of the law. First, state statutes in all states make school attendance mandatory, typically starting at age 6 or 7 and ending at age 16 or later.[6] This legal obligation rests both on the parent (enforceable either by a direct criminal prosecution or by a neglect proceeding) and on the child (who can be pursued as a truant).[7] Second, although states cannot constitutionally require attendance at a publicly run school,[8] they can establish and fund such schools and let economic reality (or civic spirit) take its course. About nine of every ten elementary or high school students in the United States attend a public school.[9] The combination of these facts—that the government requires a very large cohort of the population to participate in institutions over which the government has a near monopoly—gives school time its remarkable importance.

School time—the structure our society has established for having children spend time in school—implicates all four of the facets of social time. It allocates hours to education. It coordinates classes and other school activities so that they start and end at approximately the same time, each day and each semester. It embraces a rhythm of weekdays and weekends, Christmas holidays and spring holidays, winters and summers. And especially in the alternations of the last of these rhythms, it creates one of the most important textures of our social time, summer as we know it.

Within school time there are, naturally enough, a school year, a school week, and a school day, arranged as follows:[10]

- The school "year" consists of 180 "working" days.
- Although there are typically two or three week-long vacations within this "year," it otherwise runs straight through, so that it leaves a large gap between its end and its next beginning.
- That gap falls in the summer.

- The school "week"—so much taken for granted that the National Commission did not even address its structure[11]— contains five days, except when there is a holiday.
- These five days are Monday through Friday, leaving Saturday and Sunday as time off.

- Finally, the school "day" comprises just under six "working" hours.
- This "day," including breaks, starts fairly early in the morning and ends early in the afternoon.

In one respect this school "clock" mirrors the time displayed by other "clocks" of the society. School children "go to work" Monday through Friday, following the pattern of most, although not all, adults. Insofar as the causal connections operate the other way— insofar as many of the adults who go to work Monday through

Friday are following the pattern of their school-age children—the work week is brought closer to its paradigmatic form. In short, the school week and the work week reinforce each other. This synchronization of "weeks" highlights the fact that, in regard to the day and the year, the clock of school time is very different from the clock of work time.

How did the school year get to be 180 days long, with most of the remaining days collected in a long summer vacation? The folk wisdom is that this pattern embodies the agricultural calendar of times past. A little thought will show, however, that this cannot be the whole story. A large part of the growing season, even in northern states, falls outside of late June, July, and August, including the often labor-intensive planting and harvesting of many crops. Other forces must also have been at work.

Before the American Civil War, public education—that is, education provided at public expense although at the time not obligatory in attendance—was characterized by two very different calendars. In rural areas, schools were open at most six months of the year, half in the winter and half in the summer, with older children (who were more useful on the farm) often attending only the winter session.[12] In many urban areas, by contrast, schools were open much longer. In the early 1840s, New York's school year lasted 49 weeks, Chicago's 48 weeks; Brooklyn's was 11 months, Baltimore's the same; Philadelphia's was 251½ days, Detroit's 259 days.[13] (These are all roughly comparable figures.) Again, that does not necessarily mean either that most children attended school or that individual students attended all year. But the pattern of the calendar was that schools were open all year, often operating on the basis of four terms of 12 weeks each, with a week's vacation between terms.[14] In urban areas, then, the pre–Civil War school calendar to a large extent mimicked the calendar of commerce; in rural areas, by contrast, schools found space in the selvage left by the seasonal patterns of agriculture.

Neither pattern looks like the current calendar described by the National Commission; that, if anything, looks more like a compromise between the two.

The about-nine-month, summer-off school year was constructed in the years roughly between the Civil War and World War I.[15] No adequate history of this development has as yet been written. But it seems no coincidence that the school year as we know it developed alongside the advent of compulsory education.

Schooling required by law was first instituted in Massachusetts in 1852, but it became general in the North and West only later in the nineteenth century, and in the South only in the years just before the First World War.[16] As a matter of general social history, many factors contributed to the movement to have compulsory schooling, including the need for a more educated work force, a desire to Americanize immigrants, adult workers' fear of competition from child labor, and the pedagogical goals of school reformers. These social pressures resulted in making student attendance legally mandatory, and the choice of this mechanism had implications. Once it was a matter of law, schooling had to conform to the various formal and political constraints that our society puts on legal matters. And once it was attendance that was required, the focus of mandatory schooling was put squarely on time. (If the laws had been written in terms of attaining a mandatory competence, for example, instead of a mandatory attendance, the impact on school activities might have been far different.)

Against the background of the widely varying local educational practices of mid-nineteenth-century America, legally mandating school attendance had three possible implications for the development of the school calendar. First, once attendance was required by law, the longer the required period, the greater the requisite justification. Compulsory education obviously infringed on the freedom of both the student and the parent. It was one thing to offer schooling year-round at public expense; it was another to demand attendance. Consistent with the laissez-faire spirit of the age, there were indeed court cases in which parents claimed that compulsory education violated their rights with regard to their offspring. Consistent with the urge for social improvement also typical of the Victorian age, these claims did not prevail.[17] They did, however, reveal the mental starting point: compulsion needed to be justified. Since the longer the school year, the greater the infringement, it seems on general principle (or at least the general principle of that era) that the legislatures should have started with a presumption in favor of requiring only a short period of attendance.

The second potential implication of making education compulsory by state statute was that differences between rural and urban school calendars would start to lose their self-evident legitimacy. Mandatory education was defended in terms of social welfare: that it was good for youngsters to go to school either for their personal growth (which their parents, although normally their competent guardians, might be too benighted to recognize) or as contributing to their fitness for citizenship and productivity. (Or at least it was better for them to go to school than to go to work on a full-time basis, for compulsory education laws were closely connected with laws prohibiting child labor.)[18] Now, if education was good for children (or good for the society because it was good for children), there would be a strong argument that children everywhere should be given an equal start in life, at least insofar as state legislation required that education. This argument stood in opposition to the pre-existing diversity of school calendars, which was a product of voluntarism and localism. One could have argued, of course, that a persisting diversity of conditions justified disparate treatment: perhaps city youth were more in need of schooling than their country cousins because rural life outside of school was by itself more conducive to solid growth than life on the city streets. (Or perhaps the children of immigrants in the cities were more in need of non-parental training in "American" ways.) But the tendency of state-wide compulsion was toward uniformity.

The third implication of compulsory schooling was its possible impact on the pre-existing very long school years in urban districts. If compulsory education laws were both needed and effective, more students—requiring more teachers, more books, and more rooms—would enter the school system. Providing for those students would have a first call on resources precisely because their education was mandatory. Offering an extended school year at public expense for students (or parents) who chose it would be relegated to a lower priority. Even though compulsory education statutes stipulated only a mandatory minimum number of days, provision of that minimum could create pressure to reduce the maximum length of the public school year. If funds were scarce (hardly a counterfactual hypothesis where public education is concerned), the maximum school year would regress toward the required minimum, further reducing interdistrict differences.

In sum, making school attendance compulsory against the backdrop of very different rural and urban practices might be thought to produce three effects on the school calendar: we would expect to see the mandatory school year start short; we would expect to see it get longer over time as the impulse to equalization took hold; and we would expect to see the school year in districts with very long school years regress toward the required number of days so that the mandatory school year and the offered school year eventually became the same, or nearly so. There is indeed evidence to support this analysis. As compulsory education was implemented, the length of required schooling did grow over time and did become more congruent with the length of time when schools were actually open; meanwhile, the disparities among districts were reduced. If 180 days (36 weeks of five days, not counting holidays) represents a rough compromise between the pre-existing rural and urban standards, it was compulsory education that created the forces that made compromise happen.

We can see this dynamic at work in the particulars of the compulsory education laws as they developed. From the start, they were framed in terms of required time. The earliest compulsory education statute, a Massachusetts law of 1852—the only such statute passed before the Civil War—required children aged 8 through 14 to go to school 12 weeks a year.[19] Perhaps reflecting the fact that in some districts the school year was broken up, or that children did not attend with great regularity, the statute mandated that only 6 of the required weeks had to be consecutive.[20] And reflecting the fact that in some districts the 12-week requirement was too much, the statute also provided that 12 weeks were required only "if the public schools within such town or city shall be so long kept."[21]

Massachusetts amended its statute many times over the next fifty years; the course of those changes is revealing. In 1860, although the mandatory schooling period remained at the 12 weeks stipulated in 1852, children under age 12 could not be employed in manufacturing unless they had attended school for 18 weeks in the preceding year.[22] In 1873, the compulsory schooling period for those 8 to 12 years old, without regard to employment status, was raised to 20 weeks.[23] By 1882, thirty years after the Commonwealth first made education compulsory, the matter stood like this:

> Every person having under his control a child between the ages of eight and fourteen years shall annually cause such child to attend for at least twenty weeks some public day school in the city or town in which he resides, which time shall be divided so far as the arrangement of school terms will allow into two terms each of ten consecutive weeks.[24]

Even this 20-week period of required attendance, however, was still short of the length of time schools were open, which by law was at least six months of the year for grammar schools and ten months for high schools (although the latter were not required at all in the smallest communities).[25]

In 1890, the compulsory period in Massachusetts for children aged 8 through 14 (but not for the schools themselves) was extended to 30 weeks "if the schools are kept open that length of time."[26] Perhaps as a compromise with the need for all hands at the harvest, students were allowed "two weeks' time for absences not excused."[27] These provisions were carried forward in 1894, but with the additional proviso that "attendance shall begin within the first month of the fall term of school,"[28] which represents a first effort to synchronize the school year of the school with the school year of the student. This synchronization was carried much further in the comprehensive revision of the law passed in 1898. Grammar schools were now required to be open 32 weeks a year, and high schools (except in the smallest communities) still for 40.[29] Children aged 7 to 14 had to attend "during the entire time the public day schools are in session."[30] Or, as the point was rephrased in the statutory codification issued in 1902:

> Every child between seven and fourteen years of age shall attend some public day school in the city or town in which he resides during the entire time the public day schools are in session. . . . The attendance of a child upon a public day school shall not be required if he has attended for a like period of time a private day school. . . . Every person having under his control a child as described in this section shall cause him to attend school as herein required; and if he fails for five day sessions or ten half day sessions within any period of six months . . . , he shall . . . be punished by a fine of not more than twenty dollars.[31]

Thus by the turn of the twentieth century, the obligation to attend school in Massachusetts—32 weeks for grammar school students—had come close to the present-day requirement; at the same time, it had become congruent with—indeed was defined in terms of—the school year as measured by the length of time schools had to be open.

The statutes of New York and California, also leaders in the movement for universal and compulsory education, reveal substantially the same developments. Both passed their first compulsory education laws, applicable to children from 8 to 14, in 1874. Again the legislatures started slowly, not only in absolute terms but also with reference to the length of time schools were actually open. New York's 1874 statute required 14 weeks of attendance a year, of which only 8 had to be consecutive;[32] California's required attendance for two-thirds of the at least six months that local schools were to be open.[33] And again, over time, the required period of attendance both increased in absolute terms and became congruent with the period of school opening. As early as 1894, younger children in New York had to go to school "as many days annually, during the period between the first days of October and the following June, as the public school of the district or city in which such child resides, shall be in session."[34] Congruence between required attendance at grammar school and the at-least-six-month school year was achieved in California by 1905.[35] Thereafter, these states slowly enlarged the range of children subject to compulsory education and increased the length of the required school year: by about World War I, New York mandated 180 days per year,[36] California, 160.[37]

At the same time that state legislation was increasing the length of the mandatory minimum school year, and bringing rural districts up to a uniform standard, the maximum school year in urban areas was decreasing. As suggested earlier, this drop might have been a result of schools' having to tend not merely to a greater number of children, but also to their increased daily attendance;[38] and this in turn might have been a result of compulsory legislation.[39] But whether these causal hypotheses are valid or not, the result is clear: city school systems during the period leading up to World War I reduced the length of their over-minimum school years.[40] In his "Report for 1891–92," the U.S. Commissioner of Education compared the school years in several major American cities for 1891–92 with those of fifty years earlier. In New York, the school year had gone down from 49 weeks to 202½ days; in Chicago, from 48 weeks to 192 days; in Philadelphia, from 251½ days to 201 days. In terms of starting and stopping dates, holidays, and Saturday sessions, "the constant tendency," the Commissioner said, was "toward a reduction of the time." The supposed benefits of a shorter year in terms of better health or improved learning had, he suggested, "not . . . been clearly proved"; what was clear was that a "boy of to-day" had to go to school for 11 years to receive as much instruction as a boy had received in 8, fifty years earlier.[41] Two years later, although the text of the Commissioner's Report still spoke in terms of urban schools being open "for two hundred days of the year,"[42] the reality that he reported in his statistics was that the average city school was open 191.9 days.[43] By 1900–01, the Report showed a further drop to 187.3 days[44]—not far above present-day practice.

By World War I, as the school year got longer in the country and shorter in the city, schools considered as a whole were open for an average of 160 days a year.[45] During the 1920s, that average rose to a little over 170 days.[46] While the average continued to inch up in later years to 180 days—in some states getting to that point only recently—the structure of the current situation had already been created.

As the school year was developing its canonical length, the gap in the school year was being assigned to the summer months.

Very little is known—or at least very little has been written—about why this happened. One possibility is that the summer gap is a remnant of the much longer period, covering the entire growing season, during which older children did not go to school in rural areas prior to compulsory education. As the school year grew in length, it whittled away at both ends of this period until only the summer was left. This phenomenon perhaps explains the New York statute of 1894, quoted earlier, that at one and the same time lengthened the school year and provided for compulsion only between October 1 and June 1. On this view, the processes of lengthening the school year and of isolating the summer are really the same process—a slowly ripening series of compromises, engendered by compulsory education, between the pre-existing urban and rural school calendars.

Another possibility is that the summer gap represents, not a remnant of agricultural conditions, but a response to urban circumstances as cities became more populous and more industrial. These conditions might have included a fear that cities in the summer were especially unhealthy; the ability to heat, but not to cool or to ventilate adequately, large urban school buildings; and the likelihood that those urban workers who got vacations (which could create family time if the children were free) would get them in the summer, because their workplaces, too, could be heated but not air-conditioned. There is at least some fragmentary evidence to support this hypothesis, too.[47] Perhaps both rural and urban conditions contributed to the result, each more so in one place or another. Or perhaps educators (and legislators) simply thought that students get more than usually itchy in the summer.

By the 1920s, the diversity in school time that had typified previous decades—diversity within each state and across states—was on its way out. The minimum year, the maximum year, and the mandatory year had largely coalesced, and time off had been assigned to summer. From then on, the school year was an understood concept, a legal and cultural norm. It became a standard referent by which other aspects of social life could be, and were, timed.

What is historically created can, of course, change with history as well. The "normal" school year presents a norm that is once again open for debate in our society. Whereas opinion polls used to show very strong opposition to extending the school year,[48] we have fairly good evidence that attitudes have begun to shift.

Every year the magazine *Phi Delta Kappan,* in conjunction with the Gallup organization, conducts a poll regarding many aspects of education; sometimes there is a question regarding the length of the school year. Here is a question that was asked several times in the early 1980s, and then again in the early 1990s:

> In some nations, students attend school as many as 240 days a year as compared to about 180 days in the U.S. How do you feel about extending the public school year in this community by 30 days, making the school year about 210 days or 10 months long? Do you favor or oppose this idea?

It may be that the opening of this question is somewhat contentious, and likely to make respondents feel dissatisfied with the status quo. But while that factor might affect the magnitude of the responses (so that a 55 percent figure in favor of change might not represent a solid majority), it should not change their movement over time. And there has been movement, as the following figures show:[49]

	1982	1983	1984	1991	1992
Favor	37%	40%	44%	51%	55%
Oppose	53%	49%	50%	42%	35%
Don't Know	10%	11%	6%	7%	10%

A more recent poll simply asked whether adults favored increasing the amount of time children spend in school; it did not differentiate between extending the school year and extending the school day, but it did separate elementary school students from high schoolers. For high school, 60 percent favored more time, with 37 percent against and 3 percent uncertain; for elementary school, the results were 49 percent in favor, 48 percent opposed, and 3 percent uncertain.[50]

As a matter simply of the allocation of hours, many professional educators make the same lament we find in so many areas of life: there's not enough time. The National Education Commission on Time and Learning estimated the number of required hours of academic instruction in the last four years of schooling (that is, in what we call high school) in four countries, and found that the minimum time in the United States was less than half of what was required in Japan, France, and Germany.[51] (Or, as the Commission put the point, manhandling Commodore Perry: "We have met the enemy and they are [h]ours.")[52] This result, however, reflects not only the length of the school year, but also the length of the school day and the mix, within the school day, of academic and non-academic work. An international comparison of the standard school year in 27 jurisdictions published in 1990 showed a more varied picture. Japan at 243 school days a year topped the list, with West Germany not far behind; the Soviet Union (as it then was) came in at 211 days, the Netherlands at 200, and England at 192; and several countries besides the United States had a school year of about 180 days, including Spain, Sweden, and several Canadian provinces.[53] The United States has one of the shorter school years, but it is not unique. Indeed, the Commission's own recommendation was qualified in this regard: it was content to say that "some schools" in each district should be open year-round "so that students can find the help they need, when they need it."[54] It is hard to argue against extra help if it can be afforded; but the suggestion hardly addresses the basic structural question. Another government report, issued ten years earlier, had gone a bit further by saying that school districts and state legislatures should "strongly consider" instituting a 200- to 220-day school year.[55]

The case for a longer school year is fairly straightforward: more time will produce more learning. This is not self-evidently true, however. It may be that in some schools no learning takes place at any time or, more likely, that after nine and a half months of effort no additional learning would take place in a mandated tenth or eleventh month. Efforts to prove the claim have only yielded contested results: international measures of achievement often do not correlate closely with hours spent on a given subject.[56] There is much to be said for the proposition that what schools do to make education effective is more important than the crude number of hours allocated to children's being in school.[57] Even so, if we allow for some time for a rest between school years, it seems unlikely that the strict no-additional-benefit-from-a-longer-school-year proposition is true.

What *is* more debatable is whether the marginal benefit of 20 or 40 more days of school per year is worth the cost. These costs come in two forms, the first of which is financial. Since the school buildings are already there (although not necessarily air-conditioned), the biggest marginal cost would be additional salaries. It is unrealistic to expect teachers to work a longer year—and give up either their free time or their summer jobs—without paying them more, perhaps a good deal more. (The opposition of teachers' unions to legislative efforts to extend the school year is based, one assumes, at least in part either on the suspicion that this quid pro quo would not materialize, or on the need to establish a strong bargaining position to ensure that it does.) Perhaps 180 days is all the education that we, the taxpayers, are willing to buy—or, at least, all that we are willing to buy as members of the public, for of course alternative summer activities cost many families a great deal. The Gallup Poll numbers might look quite different if respondents were asked whether they would favor raising the tax rate in order to provide a 210-day school year.

The other "cost" of a longer school year is the number of days of each student's life it would consume. "Free time" can be wasted time, but often it is not. It may well be that certain lessons that have to be learned cannot be learned in the formal structures that typify being in school, nor tested by the formal means used for assessing academic performance. For younger children, being on a team, going to camp, or even just playing may be "teaching" valuable lessons we want our children to learn. We ought not to think of child care as comprising merely custodial arrangements to "keep kids off the street"; it can be much more. For teenagers, summer is often a time of paid employment. At that age, we need to balance our desire to keep high schoolers out of the full-time work force with our desire that they start to acquire the various disciplines of working. Americans believe in formal schooling, but only to a point—and perhaps that point is what the 180-day school year represents.

As a practical matter, there seems to be little movement toward actually enacting a school year longer than 180 days. The 1983 federal report advocating a 200- to 220-day school year was rebuffed by the states;[58] and although in the 1990s there were some state-sponsored experiments in extending the school year,[59] the longest school year mandated by any state statute is still only 186 days.[60] Perhaps the Massachusetts legislature will adopt the recent recommendation of a high-level commission of that state,[61] that children be in school 190 days a year. But whatever its educational value, a change of that magnitude would have little impact on the larger social issues involved. In the words of the former Chairman of the National Education Commission on Time and Learning which produced the report, *"Prisoners of Time* . . . has fallen on deaf ears."[62]

What are the social consequences of mandating by law a school year of 180 days? The historical writings of E. P. Thompson[63] and Michel Foucault[64] have highlighted the degree to which the structure of time constitutes an important part of the discipline exerted by many different social institutions. Nowhere is this more apparent in everyday life than in the enforcement of school time, including the school year, by the schools themselves. "Taking attendance"—the statutory mandate reduced to quotidian form—is an important school ritual. Bringing in notes from parents or physicians with reasons to excuse absences is a part of growing up. Exemplary attendance is recognized by school awards. And regular attendance is considered when promotion to a higher grade is at stake. There may be only a limited number of proceedings to enforce school time through what we ordinarily think of as legal processes—through neglect and truancy proceedings—but these apparently non-legal, yet in fact official, mechanisms do the job instead.

It is commonly understood (and sometimes dwelled upon by teachers) that this discipline is meant to carry over to the adult life of the student—is meant, that is, to instill positive attitudes toward regular attendance in later aspects of life. What is perhaps less commonly appreciated is that the enforced discipline of school time extends beyond students to affect the society as a whole. School time is a major timepiece for the whole family. The yearly rhythm of school vacations sets the boundaries within which many coordinated family activities take place—and presents a problem to be solved when parents are not free to coordinate with their young. The daily requirement of school attendance affects the daily practices of adults, too, to the extent (and it is often a considerable extent) that parents organize themselves to support their children in conforming to the discipline of the schools (by waking them up, feeding them breakfast, walking or driving them to school, collecting them after school, and so forth). And because these adults participate in other activities of the society, their practices are communicated to many other aspects of social life as well.

Indeed, while the number of days allocated to the school year may be an important educational question, the larger social questions revolve, not around the number per se, but around how this number—and the form it has taken—intersects with other aspects of social time. The issues, again, are coordination, rhythm, and texture.

Because in our society we live in families, school time inevitably rubs against work time. Although the school week and the work week are generally congruent, the school year does not fit well alongside the work year. There are 260 week days (Mondays through Fridays) in the 52 weeks that approximate a calendar year. Workers with considerable seniority operating under good union contracts might be entitled, in addition to weekends, to four weeks of vacation and a dozen other holidays, 32 work days in all.[65] This leaves even well-placed workers with a full-time work year of 228 days, which is more than nine weeks (of five days each) longer than students' school years of 180 days. No likely increase in the school year would come close to bridging that gap. Even if we adopted the European standards for vacation time urged by some writers, the basic mandate would be this same four weeks of vacation;[66] this would give many families who do not have the protection of strong work contracts more time together—a good thing—but it would not solve this fundamental structural discrepancy. Nor would any likely combination of more adult vacation and more school days.

Much of this discrepancy between school time and work time

used to be absorbed by many mothers' not working outside of the home, or working only short days and short years. Women created a "family time" which served to mediate the historically different constructs of work time and school time. With the rapid increase of women working in full-time, full-year jobs, the conflict now faces us in its unmediated form. It is not coincidental that public opinion has increasingly favored a longer school year as families in which all parents work have become more common. But the underlying structural issue presented by the history of the school year—that the school year is substantially shorter than the work year—is unlikely to change.

What might change is the way in which the 180 days of the school year are organized. Indeed, in many school districts it already has. In the academic year 2000–01, about 2.16 million students, in more than 3,000 schools located around the country but especially in California, participated in school schedules organized in a very different way.[67] They were students in what has come to be called "year-round education."

In year-round education, students still go to school for a total of 180 days, but they attend at all seasons. Instead of one long summer vacation, they get several short ones interspersed throughout the year. Several different plans have been tried. In the 45–15 plan, to take an example, students go to school for 45 week days and then are off for 15; four such cycles (allowing also for traditional holidays) constitute the year.[68] The 180-day year can also be made up of three cycles of 60 days on, 20 off; or two of 90 and 30.[69] Within these cycles, all students can be on the same schedule, or they can be split into separate cohorts. Under the 45–15 plan, to continue the example, students can be divided into four groups, with each group starting the school year 15 days later than its predecessor. If this is done, one-quarter of the students will be on vacation at any given time, and three-quarters will be in school.

As can be seen, year-round education conducted on this multiple-cohort basis in effect enlarges the capacity of school buildings. This saves money—not an enormous amount of money, since teachers still have to be paid, and books and supplies bought—but money on new construction, and to some extent on non-instructional personnel.[70] Probably this saving has been the single strongest factor leading to the adoption of year-round education, which has been of special interest to school districts with rapidly increasing school-age populations.[71] As Los Angeles describes its considerable number of year-round schools (about 240 in the school year 1998–99), they "operate on year-round multi-track schedules to accommodate overcrowded conditions by making use of school facilities throughout the year."[72]

This multiple-cohort version of year-round education is reminiscent of the "continuous production week" of the Soviet Union—and not surprisingly so, since the two share, as their basic principle of organization, the effort to stretch scarce capital resources as far as possible. Its effect is to undermine the school as an institution, or rather, to replace the school with several, perhaps four, sub-schools, differentiated by nothing more than being, let us say, 15 days apart. This creates mischief—which extends from administrators who cannot hold full faculty meetings, to students whose fellow athletic team members revolve in and out of the school, to children who are sometimes in school at the same time as their friends and sometimes not, and sometimes on vacation at the same time as their friends and sometimes not. Since sharing a rhythm helps create the group, shuffling people in and out like so many factory shifts creates a "shift identity" that undermines having a school spirit as a whole. For families with several children on different shifts within one school or especially between schools—a situation that cannot always be avoided if the schools are to be manageable within themselves—life becomes chaotic; in the words of the most detailed study of the social consequences surrounding the scheme in Los Angeles, "family time is assumed to be disruptible."[73] Similarly, if we consider the local community as a whole, when some children are always in school and some are always out, there is no public marker of the schools' social rhythm which would help coordinate adult time with school time.[74] It is perhaps not surprising that schools like these are most prevalent, at least in Los Angeles, in communities with little political power.[75]

But there are also schools that have adopted year-round education on a single-cohort basis, where, if anything, this system increases the cost of education. All students in the single-cohort version of year-round education share the same schedule, avoiding the disruptions we have just discussed. And so it is this model of year-round education that more fairly competes with the traditional school calendar.

The choice is not primarily a matter of academic performance. It is true that proponents of year-round education argue the educational superiority of their proposals. Students, they say, will forget much less during several short breaks than they now do over the long summer. Teachers, therefore, will be able to spend less time at the beginning of the semester going over old material, and will move on to more advanced material more rapidly. Proponents also argue that more frequent breaks will allow students who are falling behind to get the extra help they need before a whole year has gone by.

But school time is lost in frequently starting up and shutting down, too. Whether one long period of forgetting is better or worse than four short ones seems uncertain. Review at the beginning of a semester could as well be considered "reinforcement" as "waste." And it is not clear why a school district that could mobilize effective supplementary resources in a short break could not do so during a traditional school year on an after-school basis.

The empirical research to date does not provide a clear ground for choosing between one set of arguments and the other. In part this is because different studies have focused on year-round plans which are very different in their conception and implementation; this, as well as the researchers' own varied research designs, has made problematic any generalization from individual studies to the issue as a whole. But in part it is because different studies have in fact drawn different conclusions: in favor of year-round education, neutral, and against. What appears to be a careful survey of the literature, conducted in 1994, found that "the preponderance of evidence suggests that YRE [year-round education] students' performance on measures of academic learning (e.g., reading, math) is about the same in most studies as their performance while on traditional schedules, while some YRE programs were found to yield significantly higher student achievement scores. . . . Overall, there appears to be a slight but not overwhelming advantage for YRE students. . . . What is clear is that well-implemented YRE programs do not result in any lessening of learning."[76] Another review, made a few years earlier, took a similar position: "There are no definitive studies showing that student achievement in year-round programs differs from that of students in traditional school programs."[77] These conclusions might be of great comfort if, by reason of financial necessity, one were driven to adopt year-round education in its multi-cohort form,[78] although even here one might worry about the failure of many studies to reveal what form of year-round education they are addressing. But on the broader issue of whether schools should in general be reorganized, they are of little help.

The relevant questions are not so much about school learning, but rather about how we want our children to grow up in the larger sense of the term (which includes the many other types of things we want them to learn), and about how we as adults propose to take care of them. In the traditional calendar, all the school days are clustered in fall, winter, and spring. This pattern—fall-winter-spring "on," summer "off"—is, as we have seen, a historical creation, reflecting remnants of forces as varied as the rural school calendar and the lack of air-conditioning. Whatever its original purpose, the historical effect of this pattern has been to establish a strong rhythm in the school year by which the activities of millions of school children are coordinated with each other, and a texture by which children's lives are differentiated from those of most adults. This rhythm and differentiation appear most strongly not in the cluster of school days, but rather in the cluster of non-school days. The central issue is summer—not as understood by the scientist, but as understood by the society.

The eighty or so years during which the school calendar has been normalized at fall-winter-spring "on" and summer "off" have had wide-reaching consequences. This means more than the simple statement that being on vacation is usually fun, although that is true. Specific functional realities are embedded in current institutional arrangements. Camps are "summer camps." Full-time programs to develop athletic skills are "summer programs." Full-work-week but short-term jobs are "summer jobs." Beyond these practical matters, the alternating texture of school time and vacation time has given summer an emotional and symbolic appeal. Of course, it may be said that merely because of better weather and the fecundity of nature, summer has always been a favored time. But the tendency of modern life, as lived in offices and factories, has been to even out the months of the year. In our current circumstances it is school time, as much as anything, that restates the assumption that, because it is summer time, the living is easy.

The case for a year-round school calendar comes down to the claim, broadly speaking, that even though we are attached to this long-summer-off pattern, it does not fit present realities. Most adults work now, and few adults, the argument goes, can take extended summer vacations; in some jobs they can hardly take time off in the summer at all. Opportunities for recreation exist in the fall, winter, and spring as well as summer; in some communities, indeed, "year-round education" is called the "four-vacation plan." Recreational programs do not need to fit into the "summer camp" model, but can be offered—perhaps more easily offered— on a year-round basis. And for those for whom school is not only a place of learning but also a place where they receive social services, it may be easier to continue those services across shorter vacations than across the summer.[79]

In evaluating these claims, one must admit that for families summer is a problem as well as an opportunity. Adults on work time cannot experience summer the way children on school time can. Of course, when the workers in the family are themselves on vacation at times in the summer, having the youngsters on vacation as well enables the family as a unit to go on a trip or otherwise do things together. But such family vacations are, for everyone but the very, very lucky, very, very few, much shorter than the 10 or 12 weeks that students are out of school. For the rest of the time, the absence of school means the presence of children who need care and activity. These needs become an immediate problem for family units in which all of the adults work: two-parent families with dual careers or one-parent families with a single career. Such families have always existed, but they have become much more common in the last quarter-century.

It may fairly be asked, in other words, whether the school year as we know it depends on an assumption—no longer nearly as true as it once was—that during the summer a caregiving parent will be at home. Problems of family coordination when all the adults are at work and the children are out of school can be intense. A very large block of time has to be covered, and almost no single alternative—not even the most extended of private camps—will cover it all. Parents who work inevitably have to put together a pastiche of arrangements. Especially for younger children, the situation may involve a play group here, a child-care provider there, a relative for part of the time, a one-week or two-week program, parents' vacation time, and perhaps some personal leave days for one or both parents, until September finally comes again.

But it is a mistake to think that the fundamental difficulty here is the collection of non-school days into a single long vacation period. The difficulty, rather, is the different length—the considerably different length—of the school year and the work year. This problem is unlikely to go away. Year-round education, despite its name, does not change the basic point. It could indeed be argued that 180 school days on a year-round basis represents the worst of both worlds, not the best. The particular rhythm of summer is gone, and students' lives more closely resemble those of their parents. But parents are still unlikely to be free from work for most of the 12 weeks during which their children are not in school; and now there are four distinct periods in which alternative arrangements must be made. Moreover, the chance for a substantial alternative experience for the children—including a substantial work experience—is now gone.

In truth, which arrangement is most convenient seems highly dependent on context: geography, socioeconomic class, and purely personal circumstances all play a part.[80] In regard to arranging care, for some children there are relatives happy to have the child for a week or two at a time, but not for the whole summer; for others, there are formal child-care arrangements more easily made once than many times; and for quite a number of children, the way the vacations arise will also determine how they spend time with a distant, separated parent. In regard to alternative uses of vacation time, some children participate in serious summer programs, or have substantial summer jobs, and some do not;

some communities will succeed in developing innovative uses for the shorter vacations of year-round calendars, and some will not; in some neighborhoods children can be safely sent out to play by themselves for a length of time, and in some not. One might think that older children are more likely to make productive use of the long summer, and that this fact favors using year-round schedules in elementary school, with traditional schedules thereafter. Indeed, year-round education is more common in elementary schools. But compromising in this fashion only further fragments the family time of those with more than one child. Perhaps because the matter depends on such a great variety of circumstances, when a change of school calendar is bruited in a community, fireworks often result; superintendents have been heard to say that only racial integration is more contentious. But opinion polls tend to support the generalization that most (but not all) people adapt to such a change, and, having adapted, tend to favor the status quo in their community, whatever it is.[81] Taken all in all, the argument of the reformers, that school time should become year-round because it will fit better with work time, is no more powerful than its opposite.

Considered in other terms, the fact that the established school year differs substantially from the ordinary work year provides the strongest argument for *not* changing it. Differentiated time creates differentiated meanings. The maintenance of summer in the sense that we have been examining—summer as time off—is the best way we have of saying, in a tangible and forceful way, that working is not all there is to life. "Summer" represents a judgment of the proper balance of life.

We are, perhaps, not used to periods of time having special meanings. Traditionally, however, the presence within the same society of both Sabbath days and work days stood as a recognition that there is more than one side to life. In our society, the religious differentiation of time does not have the force it once had.

But it is still important to assert the principle that living is not synonymous with working; and it is still true that a powerful way to do this is by differentiating time. "Summer" as a construct of school time is a period with a strong, largely positive cultural valence, and summer in this sense is not a remnant of ancient history. Although it cannot be said that the school year was created with an intention to differentiate time, we are unlikely to create an equally powerful alternative pattern starting from scratch anytime soon. With the power of Sunday on the wane, the still-vibrant rhythm of school time is now the most powerful rhythm we have with which to counter the rhythm of work time. It is this truth that should make us want to maintain "summer" for our children, by which we will also maintain at least the suggestion of summer for ourselves. This does not mean that we can expect parents to stop working in the summer, or that we can ignore the need as a society to provide for children's needs and care during the summer. What it does mean is that we should try to bridge the gap between the school year and the work year in a way that embraces their difference rather than in a way that tries to deny it. What we need to work on is providing all children with worthwhile activities in the summer—which probably will require us to move beyond relying as much as we do on the private provision of opportunities—rather than doing away with this texture of time.

The other feature by which school time differs from work time is the length of the school day. The story of the school day resembles that of the school year. The roughly 5½ hours of classroom time per day reported by the National Education Commission on Time and Learning emerged as the dominant pattern during the post–Civil War period, and is an hour or so shorter than the school day typical of pre–Civil War urban schools.[82] State law, either by statute or by administrative regulation, typically sets a required minimum number of hours per year, while local school boards determine the actual starting and ending times for the day.

There is some tendency to require more hours for secondary than for elementary students.[83] The actual starting times are often earlier for high school than for elementary school students: high schoolers are more likely to have athletic practice, or jobs, to be fit in after school, and are more able to care for themselves during the dark hours of winter mornings. Staggered schedules are especially important in school districts where students are bused, so that drivers and vehicles can make more than one run. "Lateness" is an infraction against a school discipline meant to establish a general structure for social experience.

Many educators favor lengthening the school day, at least in the sense that they advocate reserving the existing 5½ hours for core academic subjects; if the schools are to continue doing the other things they do, the length of the overall school day would have to grow.[84] The general population, however, is not very enthusiastic about lengthening the school day. In the 1993 Gallup Poll, forced to choose a method of increasing school time, 47 percent of respondents voted to increase the number of days, while 33 percent voted to make each day longer. (5 percent would hold Saturday morning classes, and the rest either would combine the schemes or had no view.)[85] These results may reflect several things: a strong sense that children tire out by the end of the day, and deserve to play; the importance attributed to extracurricular activities held after school, or to part-time employment; and the increasing availability of end-of-day child-care programs, many of them held on school premises. Perhaps because of these views, perhaps because of practical problems, the educators' proposals have met with only limited success.

The upshot is that through the different processes by which society has created the work day and the school day, the current school day has become and will remain shorter than the normal work day. This creates obvious problems of coordination for most modern families. There are numerous ways of filling the gap: some children look after themselves; some work part-time; some are cared for by an adult outside their home; some are enrolled in structured, purposeful programs. For reasons similar to (but probably less intense than) those given a few pages ago regarding the discrepancy between the school year and the work year, there is a lot to be said for continuing to structure after-school activities as something other than "school" itself. There is a great need to increase the social provision of after-school opportunities, and in recent years there has been some real movement to address that need.

But what also needs to be done—and here there has been barely a glimmer of social recognition—is to attend to the ending time of the work day, which is to say, to the other end of the school day / work day gap. This is not just a matter of the number of hours parents work, but of how those hours are structured. For many parents, the central point is to increase their control over—or at least their ability to rely on the regularity of—the end of the work day, for having this control is the prerequisite to making sensible provision for covering the gap between their days and their children's.

As we shall now see, the law helps structure this aspect of social life, too.

6

Disputes at the Boundaries of Time

Social time, as we have seen, is not made up of undifferentiated minutes. Chunks of time are organized so that the efforts of many people can be coordinated with each other; so that groups can establish the rhythms that help maintain both their activities and the groups themselves; and so that different meanings can be assigned to periods of time for various culturally significant purposes. The specifics of any particular pattern are, of course, open to debate, but that there ought to be some such organization is beyond doubt. In particular, in a society such as ours in which we expect individuals to play many different social roles in a variety of social settings, it is desirable that there be many different organizations of time to support these various activities.

If we now consider the same situation from the point of view of the individual, we see that as a person moves through life—or even through a single day—he or she constantly crosses temporal "boundaries," the edges of these various agglomerations of time. (Often the individual crosses a boundary in space, too: "going to work" is at the same time a transposition from home to factory or office, and from family time to work time.) Because each of these constellations has its own internal dynamic, there is no guarantee that their boundaries will fit smoothly one with another.

Of course, not everyone crosses the same boundaries, or boundaries with the same rigidity. There have always been individuals, for example, who worked for their living at home, merging to some extent their work time and their family time. Traditionally these have included farmers, artisans, and writers; perhaps today we are more familiar with professionals who telecommute for part or all of their work time. But the common experience is that there are borders to cross, and that there is often tension at the borders.

Emblematic of these difficulties are the problems that lie at the boundaries of work time, and especially at the line between work time and family (or personal) time (which for many people involves the boundaries of school time as well). Even when things are going well, there is pressure: in the morning, everyone has to wash, dress, and eat, and the children have to be sent off to school, or arrangements made for an elderly member of the household, so that the working adults can get to work on time; at the end of the day, work has to be finished up so that someone can care for the children or the elderly, and so that everyone can gather together to reestablish family time in the evening.

What happens when things do not go well? Boundary disputes can then become matters of legal dispute, too. What is the law of being late to or absent from work? Does it matter if the cause is caring for a sick child? Who decides whether an employee must work overtime (even if compensated at a premium rate)? Does it matter if the employee has conflicting family responsibilities? When can employees insist upon taking personal leave (even if it is unpaid)? Again, does it matter if the leave is to care for a member of the family? In the answers to these questions lie, not only specific rules of law, but a whole additional set of mechanisms by which the law shapes our social uses of time.

Most of the laws we have already considered—the Fair Labor Standards Act, the compulsory school attendance laws, and even the Blue Laws in those states where they are still on the books—specify mandatory rules that private parties, even if they are in agreement, are not free to vary. For example, the FLSA provides that employees who work more than 40 hours in a week must be paid time-and-a-half; it is clearly the law that even if employees and employers sign a different contract, calling only for straight time for overtime, the statutory rule will still apply and can be enforced by the Department of Labor, or by a disgruntled employee after the fact. By contrast, most of the rules governing boundary disputes about work time can be varied by the parties. What the law does is to set a baseline norm, establishing the rule that applies if the parties have not agreed otherwise, and then looks at what, if anything, the parties have written or said, to see if they have indeed stipulated something different. Thus, it can at one and the same time be "the law" that employers can require employees to work overtime and also be "the law" that the workers at a particular company have negotiated an enforceable contract that gives them the right to refuse. From a practical point of view, the "rights" established by law are only the beginning of the story, not its end.

Despite the tentative nature of these baseline norms, they are very important. As a statement of our public understanding about time, what the law considers the baseline to be has considerable moral force. Moreover, as a practical matter, many parties will not bother, or will not be able, to negotiate arrangements different from the legally implied background terms. Finally, the bulk of the law on matters arising from boundary disputes is to be found, not in the statute books, but in the decisions of courts and arbitrators resolving specific controversies. In reaching their judgments, courts and arbitrators rely not only on facts particular to the parties, but also on their general understanding of the proper relationship between employees and employers. Thus, even when there is a contractual term that applies to a case, courts and arbitrators often read such terms narrowly, in order not to disturb their basic understanding of the justice of the situation.[1]

The starting point for any consideration of legal norms surrounding work time is the fact that the law accords most workers no tenure in their jobs, unless they can point to a specific agreement to the contrary. Instead, the law characterizes them as employees-at-will, who can quit or be fired for any reason at all, as long as it is not a specifically prohibited reason. For these workers, unless they can show that their discharge was really the result of sexual harassment, racial discrimination, or the like—or perhaps that it violated a company handbook—the issue of when they can be discharged for lateness or absence, or disciplined for refusing overtime, is swallowed by the general discretion accorded their employer.[2] Of course, employees-at-will can also quit when they want to, if they find that the demands of their families make it impossible to fulfill the demands of their employers. So both parties have a weapon that can be used to bargain with, or discipline, the other. At times, market conditions give workers great bargaining power and consequent flexibility—as was true, for example, for many computer-savvy employees throughout the 1990s. It does not, however, require sophisticated sociological proof to show that in the usual employer-employee relationship, this formal evenhandedness works more to the advantage of the employer—that in most instances the employee needs this particular job more than the employer needs this particular worker. In many cases, then, the law at the boundary between work time and family time is simply that the employer's rules control the situation.

To get further aid from the law, the employee must be able to show something more than just an employment relationship— some additional restraint on the employer's power to control the boundary. Thus, to explore further the law at the boundary between work time and family time, we have to look for employees who have some additional claim to having their domestic circumstances count—workers who can be fired only if their employer has "cause" or "just cause" to do so. These employees include many government workers protected by civil service statutes, teachers who have "tenure," and employees who work under union contracts. Virtually all collective bargaining agreements include an "only-for-cause" dismissal provision.[3]

We can start with the most mundane boundary between work time and other time—the question of workplace attendance. Under what circumstances does the tardiness or absence of employees furnish "just cause" for their discipline or ultimate dismissal?

Most of the law on this subject resides in the reports of labor arbitrators appointed by the parties to determine rights under collective bargaining agreements. Many of the cases subject the employer's power of discharge to restrictions designed to ensure that the process of discharge is fair. Labor arbitrators commonly take into consideration, for example, whether the employee had notice of the company's required standard of attendance, whether the standard was applied uniformly, and whether the employee had some initial warning that future infractions might lead to serious consequences. Another consideration is the seriousness of the sanction in proportion to the employee's lapses; what will justify a short suspension will not necessarily sustain the harsh remedy of discharge. Arbitrators also—and this is more relevant to the substance of the social situation—often look at the reasonableness of the substance of the employer's rules, and of any excuse tendered by the employee as a justification.[4]

Why do employers want to enforce rules regarding absenteeism or tardiness? The most obvious reason is that there is work to be done, and often it has to be done at, or within, a specific time. Sometimes an answering machine will do, but often the phone has to be answered during commonly accepted business hours, not just whenever-you-please. Another important reason is that the work that has to be done often requires the synchronization or coordination of the efforts of many workers; the failure of some to appear wastes the diligence of others. It is no good having the flight attendants and copilot on board the plane and ready to go, if the pilot is still asleep in bed. In addition, it is probably true that employers wish, by enforcing rules regarding time, to exert their authority and set a tone of discipline in a more general sense. It is not just school teachers who think that precise attention to time, and maintenance of a rhythm of routine, generate greater attention to the task.

We must also ask why some employees are absent or late to work more than is common. Perhaps they lack internal discipline and the ability to organize their lives. Perhaps they are the victims of bad luck and suffer from chronic illness. Perhaps they are dependent on unreliable public transportation. Perhaps they live in other circumstances in which unusual efforts are needed to bring their own lives into congruence with the tempos of the workplace. Perhaps they have obligations to family members to which they have to give priority at times. Perhaps they hate their jobs. Or perhaps they are just more free-spirited than the rest of us.

Which of these reasons—or of the many other possible ones on both sides—should be taken into account? As a matter of common morality, we accept a rather large number of reasons as excuses for lateness or absence, at least in non-work settings. No one would blame parents for being late to, or absent from, a party because a child was sick. But at work, say the arbitrators, the focus is different. It is not a matter of blame and punishment; it is a matter of an employee's failing to live up to a bargain and an employer's need to manage its business. In short, employees can be fired for persistent absence or lateness caused by forces quite beyond their control.[5]

The extreme case is provided by what are called "no-fault" attendance programs, which have become increasingly common since the 1970s.[6] Under these programs, various penalty points are assigned for lateness and for absence, with perhaps a greater penalty if the employee fails to call in to give notice. If the employee accumulates a certain number of points within a given period, he or she gets a warning, followed, if further points accumulate, by progressively more severe sanctions, and ultimately by dismissal. What counts as a lateness or absence? Some things are excluded: vacation days, obviously; jury duty or military leave; perhaps funeral leave as provided by the union contract; or maybe some other items.[7] But typically such plans cover almost all latenesses and absences.

For example, "S." was discharged by the Georgia-Pacific Corporation for accumulating 17 points in a twelve-month period, calculated as follows:

> During the . . . year he was late for work on five occasions (2.5 points), absent due to sickness in his family on four occasions (2 points), sick on five occasions (3.5 points), failed to report to work on one occasion (2 points), off duty accident on one occasion (1 point), and absent without leave on twelve occasions, which was reduced by the Company to two occasions (6 points).[8]

Probably common morality would consider some of the above reasons—such as being absent without leave—blameworthy; some—tending to sickness in the family—praiseworthy; and some—such as personal sickness—to be neither one or the other; but they all count toward the final total. Although there is some differentiation of points according to grievousness, points accumulate—true to the "no-fault" moniker—regardless of whether the employee ought to be, in some other frame of reference, excused or held to account.

And what do the arbitrators say about such plans? It is often somewhat hard to state just what the arbitrators' law is on a particular subject; because each individual arbitration construes a specific contract in light of the customs of a particular workplace or industry, and because the decisions of arbitrators are only very rarely reviewable in court, the decisions often present more a series of possible answers than a definitive rule. But while some arbitrators have suggested that "the concept of just cause can never be reduced to a simple exercise in counting,"[9] a great many have said the opposite: if there is sufficient notice and if appropriate discipline procedures are faithfully followed, "S." can be lawfully dismissed.[10] Partly these arbitrators have been influenced by the apparent evenhandedness of such programs in application. Dismissal is based on objective criteria that are neither dependent on the favor of a particular manager nor subject to inconsistent application. But primarily they have justified "no-fault" plans on the basis of an inherent right of companies to manage their businesses: lateness and absence, whatever their cause, disrupt business and impose extra burdens on other employees, and management has a right to establish policies to curb them.[11]

The practical impact of a "no-fault" program depends, of course, on how strict the policy is, and this varies from plan to plan. Implicit in acceptance of the approach in any guise, however, is an assumption that it is legitimate for companies, as far as the use of time is concerned, to separate themselves from their larger social context. Perhaps from a social point of view it is important for workers to live balanced lives; perhaps from a social point of view it is not only excusable but desirable for adults to stay home with sick children; but needs like that do not have to be concerns of employers. They can, consistent with their own contractual agreement that they will fire workers only for "just cause," adopt standards of absenteeism or lateness that address only the time needs of the workplace.

Indeed, this analysis holds even for some of the decisions that have rejected "no-fault" plans as being overly mechanical. For example, "C." was discharged under a no-fault plan when, after various warnings, she continued to be absent more than 8 percent of the time. This application of a flat rule, said the arbitrator, might be useful in deciding which employees should get warnings, but when it came to a discharge under a "just cause" standard, such a "mechanical formula" would not do.[12] But what other facts should be considered? The opinion emphasized that C.'s rate of absenteeism had been falling, that some of her medical problems had been successfully treated (so there was hope that her record would continue to improve), and that she had been with the company for ten years with an otherwise good work record. Mentioned in passing, but not relied on in any way to C.'s benefit, was the fact that many of her absences were caused by one of her two children being sick, or by their having doctor's appointments. The arbitrator did not want a mechanical test, but the additional facts he wanted to consider had more to do with the fairness of the penalty of discharge considering C. as an employee, than with a balancing of the alternative claims on C.'s time pertaining to her other social roles.[13]

The import of this body of law regarding discharge for lateness or absenteeism under a collective bargaining agreement can be seen by comparing it with the parallel body of law regarding eligibility for unemployment compensation. A discharged worker is, of course, eligible for unemployment benefits, but in most states eligibility is conditional on the worker's not having been fired for (in the typical statutory formulations) "misconduct" or "willful misconduct." If the causes for an employee's discharge were lateness and absenteeism—as contrasted, say, with theft from an employer—in what situations is "misconduct" found?

Courts applying unemployment compensation statutes do require employees to take their jobs seriously: persistent absenteeism and lateness without excuse are often held to constitute misconduct sufficient to justify denying benefits to the discharged worker.[14] This is especially true when the employee has been specifically warned that his or her course of behavior is not acceptable.[15] But, consistent with the idea that unemployment compensation is a benefit, not a wage—and with the understanding that statutory language such as "misconduct" or "willful misconduct" connotes some sort of fault—the time needs of employees are also taken seriously. Mere accumulation of a number of absences or latenesses, or of points under a "no-fault" scheme, does not in itself show that an employee is not entitled to benefits.[16] Lateness or absence due to personal illness, or (especially in the more recent cases) due to the need to care for family members, are routinely (although not always) held to be sufficient excuses to negate charges of misconduct.[17] True, workers are held to some diligence in terms of process, and courts do deny benefits in situations of personal illness or family need when workers fail to notify their employers of their impending absence, or cannot document their claimed illness, or the like.[18] But the central principle of these cases seems to be that sometimes the time demands of other realms of life can legitimately take precedence over the time demands of work.

At least this is true to the extent of getting unemployment benefits. Of course, getting benefits falls far short of having a job. In terms of incentives for behavior, for most people the threat of being fired surely overpowers the opportunity to gain unemployment compensation. Thus, the more powerful rules, in terms of social structure, are those that say that the employer's needs are the basis for determining "just cause," and those that, indeed, construe most employment relationships as employment "at-will."

What about overtime? Can workers refuse to work overtime? Can they do so when they have a strong claim of need for family time? We have already seen that the answer for employees at-will, such as Johanna Upton, is no.[19] When we turn to the question of unionized workers who can be discharged only for "just cause," however, the situation is more complex. For one thing, by force of their collective bargaining agreements and the Fair Labor Standards Act, wage workers generally get premium pay for overtime. For many workers, depending on their circumstances, a moderate amount of overtime is not a curse but rather a benefit to be fairly distributed. For another thing, many union contracts—according to a recent survey, 33 percent of collective bargaining agreements—stipulate explicit rules regarding acceptance of overtime work. Of those, 47 percent allow the employer to require overtime, 42 percent make its acceptance voluntary, and 11 percent make it voluntary except in case of emergency.[20] In any of these situations, "the law" consists of interpretation of these agreements and a willingness to enforce them.

When the union contract does not explicitly address the matter, arbitrators usually rule that management has the right to require an employee to work overtime, and to discipline him for "insubordination" if he refuses.[21] At the same time, management must respect reasonable excuses.[22] The overall impact of these dual rules clearly depends on what counts as a "reasonable" excuse.

The desire to protect purely personal time does not count. In the words of one arbitrator: "When an employee is asked to work overtime, he may not refuse merely because he does not like to work more than eight hours, does not need the extra money, or for no reason at all."[23] This can be true even when the notice of overtime is very abrupt.[24]

But what happens when the employee tenders an excuse that has greater social substance? In many cases arbitrators have acknowledged the importance of run-of-the-mill needs or obligations: actual (even if not extreme) illness,[25] a pending appointment with a doctor,[26] and even a need to get a ride home.[27] But such excuses are not per se sufficient; the determination that they are "reasonable" requires comparison of the employee's needs with the company's. And this, in the end, turns on the weight given to the different claims by the arbitrators—with the consequence, as noted earlier, that the cases go in more than one direction.

The general trend of this ping-pong—employer demands overtime; employee tenders excuse; employer claims excuse is not sufficient; arbitrator compares the claims—can, however, be seen in several recent decisions of arbitrators which turn on the tension between overtime demands and child care in the context of two-job families. In each case, an employee was disciplined by his or her employer (with varying degrees of severity) for leaving the job to attend to children in the face of a demand to work overtime. The worker had failed, said management, to try hard enough to get alternative coverage.

In *Piedmont Airlines, Inc.,*[28] a flight attendant was ordered to work overtime after other attendants had called in sick. She refused to serve another flight because she would then get home after the time when her babysitter had to leave her two very young children alone. In her testimony, the attendant admitted that if a weather emergency had kept her from coming home on time, she would have arranged for a neighbor to look after the children, or arranged for her husband to come home early. She ought, said the arbitrator in upholding her disciplinary suspension, to have explored the same possibilities when told to work overtime.[29]

In *Ashland Oil, Inc.,*[30] a carpenter's failing was his walking off the job after working some overtime, in order to pick up his two children, aged 5 and under, when their day-care center closed at 5:30 P.M.; his wife also worked. "It was established," the arbitrator wrote, "that the day-care center would have continued to care for the children after its normal closing hour by only charging overtime. It was also established that he wouldn't have been much more than an hour late if he had stayed . . . and helped . . . build the two scaffolds. It was shown that the Company's need for his services was greater than his need to leave."[31]

Perhaps the drift of these cases is most pithily stated in *Southern Champion Tray Co.*:

> Accepting for sake of argument that an employee could legitimately leave work if necessary to protect a child, it does not follow that every familial problem justifies disobeying direct orders. At the very least, the employee must *try* to satisfy his or her parental obligations without interfering with the employer's business. If all attempts fail, the family must come first, as most employers would readily agree. On the other hand, if the employee indicates from the start that he does not intend to obey the order and makes no effort to resolve the problem short of disobedience, he may not then stand behind the shield of his family.[32]

In short, once asked to work overtime, employees must try diligently to satisfy their family's time needs while they stay on the job. The practical consequence of the standard of "reasonableness" applied to excuses is that the time needs of the employer become the time needs of the employee, unless that would create an emergency. The perceived risk is that family time will be "interfering" with work time, not the other way around. The bottom line—"If all attempts fail, the family must come first"—is by its own terms a strange way of coming first. The presumptive rhythm is the rhythm of work, even when the work rhythm is the rhythm of overtime.

The unemployment insurance cases concerning overtime fit the same conceptual pattern.[33] Refusal of overtime can constitute "misconduct," or perhaps a "voluntary quit," and thus undermine the claim to benefits. Here again, a balancing of the reasonableness of the employee's excuse against the employer's demand is the rule. An employee who simply refuses to work overtime without giving a reason loses his or her benefits on the theory (in the words of an Arizona appellate court) that "the refusal of a reasonable order undermines the employer's authority and, thus, interferes with the functioning of the business."[34] But, for reasons similar to those stated in the discussion of lateness and absenteeism, the unemployment compensation cases are in general more favorable to the employee. An employee can get benefits on a lesser showing than is required to justify reinstatement.[35] Again, however, getting unemployment compensation is hardly the equivalent of a job.

A broader view of what is happening in these cases at the boundary between family time and work time can be gained if we put side by side the law governing when lateness and absenteeism give "just cause" for discharge and the law governing when refusal to accept overtime gives "just cause." An employer is entitled to have its employees present and on time, unless they have a good excuse—and, if it establishes a no-fault program, even if they do have a good excuse. We might defend the law's embracing this approach on the general ground that the whole society has an interest in work getting done. Since work time functions to coordinate the work group and to give it a productive rhythm, some formality in the maintenance of the boundaries of work time is essential. But if this is true, we should then have trouble with the idea that an employer is entitled to demand overtime work from its employees, even at the expense of the employees' other responsibilities, unless they have an excuse that outweighs the employer's need. For it would seem that the whole society also has an interest in seeing to it that these other responsibilities are met, and that some formality in the maintenance of the boundaries of family time is essential to protecting this interest. Employees, on this view, should be entitled to say that home time is home time on the same principle that employers say work time is work time. "I have to pick my kids up from day care because that is what I and they do at the end of each day" would state a presumptive claim to having work time cease. It would assert the need of the family to be a coordinated unit and to maintain its own rhythm. Precisely because emergency child-care arrangements undermine this rhythm and coordination, they would be understood as inferior. We might even understand family time as a time when children come to expect their parents to "be around" even if there is no specific activity to be addressed. This is not to say that there would never be workplace emergencies that had to be met, but rather that the benefits and costs to be measured would be understood far differently.

Nor is the issue limited to the protection of family time, although that is what the cases have focused on. Having to work unplanned evenings or weekends serves to "unplan" all sorts of other activities, some of them frivolous, but many of significant social value. Of course, evening meetings can be missed or replanned. But there is a point at which constant rearranging becomes the nuisance that kills participation, and in any case there is a disruption of rhythm that undermines the importance of what is being done. It is no secret that control of time signals social priority,[36] and that "having to work" is coming out ahead of other possible "have to's." In the end, it may be easier to flop in front of the always-available TV than to try to participate in voluntary clubs and organizations that require coordination with others—even though, from the point of view of society, the social capital built through participation is very important.[37]

That this pattern raises a general issue can be shown by its replication in yet a third body of law, having to do with the scheduling of work shifts. A change in work shifts can be very disruptive of employees' family time, and of their participation in any other organized group: social, civic, or religious. As a union argued in an early case challenging management's right to institute rotating shifts, such changes are highly destructive of "a stable and normal pattern of living."[38] Nonetheless, "setting the time when employees work is usually considered to be a management right unless it is specifically altered by the written contract."[39] Arbitrators generally have upheld management's right to change the number of shifts, to institute or alter the rotation of shifts, and to change (subject to obligations to pay overtime) from a five-day work week to a six-day or seven-day schedule.[40] Meanwhile, the recent unemployment compensation cases concerning this issue point somewhat in a more employee-friendly direction. When management requires an employee to change shifts, and family duties are threatened, there is (in the words of a recent case) "an emergent majority rule against disqualification [from benefits] when a claimant quits or is discharged from employment for inability to arrange child care during [the new] working hours,"[41] although once again the employee must first make a reasonable effort to find help.[42]

In looking at these several lines of cases, we find that when only public unemployment benefits are at stake, time needs other than work are legitimated or at least recognized, but when the employment relationship per se is at issue, work time generally gets to set the tempo. It might be tempting to rationalize this as representing the difference between public policy and the private bargain; if it is a question of limiting a private employer, let employees or their union bargain for what they want. But that distinction fails to account for the fact that the background rule in employment relations is not merely that the parties can bargain about work shifts or overtime arrangements, but that if the parties fail to strike an explicit bargain, then the employer gets to set most of the rules. In the arbitration cases we have been examining, the contract most likely states that management has a right to run the business and that the employee can be discharged only for cause. From this total or near-total silence on the specific issues, it is the arbitrators who develop the default rules that make the employer's time needs part of the deal, but the employee's time needs beyond the scope of the agreement. Management gets control of the boundaries for free, just by being management; workers must offer something in exchange to get control for themselves. The law is taking a stand. And these results come from cases concerning the best protected of employees, those who can only be discharged for cause. Those who are employees at-will can only be further away from having power to control the boundary line between work time and family time.

This tilt of the law may simply be a reflection in the cases of a larger lack of symmetry in social power between employers and employees. But since we are talking in large part about the decisions of labor arbitrators chosen jointly by unions and management, there is some reason to doubt that this straightforward power hypothesis explains everything. Another possibility is that the rules we have been examining developed from the world of the one-worker/one-non-worker family, in which the boundary between work time and family time was cushioned by the availability of the non-working partner. Yet another explanation may be that the rules reflect a cultural blindness which views work time as a distinct form floating in a sea of formless, residual time—as in the formulation "work and leisure"—rather than seeing that work time shares boundaries with social, civic, and family times that need to have an integrity of their own.

Whatever the correct causal hypothesis may be, the need for reform is clear. We need to establish these other kinds of time as being more than the mere allocation of residual minutes. We need to recognize that we no longer have a large number of adult non-workers who can mediate the boundaries. And we need to understand that society must intervene to correct imbalances of power if these are preventing the maintenance of family, civic, religious, and other forms of group time.

One might think that the road to legal reform would start with the two doctrines at the center of the matter: the presumptive characterization of employment relationships as being "at will," and the interpretation, for those with some job protection, of "for cause" as still allowing for such a great breadth of managerial control. For a time in the 1970s and early 1980s, some courts flirted with the abolition of the at-will rule, which was itself a judicial creation from the previous century. But the movement fizzled out far short of gaining for non-unionized employees some "for cause" right to their jobs. Perhaps the judges sensed that making such a far-reaching change, which in addition to affecting control over time would have a general impact on the flexibility of labor markets, was beyond their mandate as jurists and should be left to the legislature. Whatever the cause, the courts nowadays will move against discharges that can be seen as harassment, or as retaliation for exercising an otherwise existing right, and they will often enforce clauses in employer-issued employee handbooks; but all of that will rarely affect the structuring of time that we have been looking at here. We are left with the interpretation of explicit "for cause" contracts, which has remained largely with arbitrators operating under collective bargaining agreements. Here, too, the results favor the protection of work time. Perhaps the arbitrators also feel role-constrained, leaving protection of family time to the next bargaining session between union and management.

Of course, the overall situation would change if there were a new wave of unionization and if more unions were willing to bargain specifically for employees' having rights to protect family time. Although there has been some movement here, it has not been, at least as yet, far-reaching. Or the several legislatures could choose generally to protect employees from discharge except for cause. But only one state—Montana—has done so,[43] and there is little reason to think that the political balance will shift in such a way that many states will follow in the near future.

As a result, instead of an overall shift in the structure of the employment relationship, what we have seen—and probably can expect to see—is a series of specific attempts to reallocate the power to organize time in particular circumstances. Probably the most important, and best known, statute intended to increase worker control at the boundaries of work time is the federal Family and Medical Leave Act (FMLA),[44] passed in 1993. Based in part on a finding that "the lack of employment policies to accommodate working parents can force individuals to choose between job security and parenting,"[45] the Act was intended, again in Congress' words, "to balance the demands of the workplace with the needs of families."[46]

The actual rights established by the FMLA are, however, narrower than Congress' language would suggest. The Act targets only certain specific "needs of families." Employees are entitled to take leave in case of their own serious illness or in case of certain serious family responsibilities: to care for an immediate relative who is seriously ill, or for a newborn or newly adopted child in the first year of its membership in the family.[47] For these purposes, workers can take up to 12 work-weeks of leave during a 12-month period. The general need or desire to care for a child throughout its early infancy—or to provide elder care on a continuing basis—is not protected. Moreover, only some workers are covered. The statutory "eligible employee" has to have worked for his or her employer for at least a year, and must be well over a half-time worker; in addition, probably of greater consequence, the statutory "employer" only covers those who employ 50 or more workers.[48] Finally—a considerable finally—although an employee may elect to take accrued paid vacation leave, personal leave, or family leave (or, indeed, an employer may require the employee to use up such paid leave), the leave mandated by the Act itself is unpaid.[49]

While the FMLA thus has only a limited scope, within that scope it evinces a stance distinctly different from the otherwise-existing legal rules. The basic attitude of the legislation is that the employer must accommodate the employee. This is apparent from the basic structure of the Act: its stipulation that eligible employees have an entitlement to 12 work-weeks of leave,[50] coupled with its prohibition on any employer's denying or interfering with the exercise of that right,[51] and backed by its generous provision of damages for infringement of that right.[52] The fact that the FMLA strikes a new balance—a balance in which the employer's interests are the subsidiary, not the dominant, consideration—shows also in the Act's details. For example, the Act's general rule is that, on the employee's return from leave, the employer must place the employee back in his or her former position, or a full equivalent; the only exception is for the highest-paid 10 percent of employees, and even then only if keeping the job open would have caused "substantial and grievous economic injury" to the employer.[53] In contrast to the background law, here the employer must make a considerable accommodation to the employee's emergency situation.

Of course, it is one thing to say that workers faced with family emergencies—or, if having a new child is not properly called an "emergency," then faced with family situations calling for suddenly increased amounts of time—should be able to get their work time rearranged. It is quite another thing to say that in general workers should have more control over the boundaries of their work time.

This more general question has been raised by the efforts made over the years, in one state legislature or another, to give workers (including non-unionized workers) greater power to refuse management's demands for overtime work.[54] It is not easy, it turns out, to draft a statute that would properly balance the considerations at stake. Consider, for example, a proposed rule saying: "no worker need work overtime unless he or she voluntarily agrees to do so." We are immediately met with the problem that a single indispensable worker can, perhaps for no good reason at all, prevent a whole production line, and a whole group of willing co-workers, from dealing with an emergency. We might meet this objection by qualifying the rule to say: "except in the case of an emergency." But then we face the problem that what constitutes an "emergency" depends greatly on the prior decisions of management. A company that is too leanly staffed will have more "emergencies" requiring existing employees to work overtime than will one with adequate personnel. To meet this objection, we might add yet another clause: "which occurs despite reasonable efforts to prevent its occurrence." But now we have a rule—"no worker need work overtime unless he or she voluntarily agrees to do so, except in the case of an emergency which occurs despite reasonable efforts to prevent its occurrence"—which, while perhaps very sensible, is quite hard to put into operation as a legal rule. The after-the-fact determination by a court of what constituted "an emergency," not to mention what constituted "reasonable efforts to prevent its occurrence," very likely will involve a review of the whole working pattern of the operation.

Moreover, if courts failed to make good judgments, this law could have implications not only for the allocation of overtime, but for the general efficiency of firms. The courts might, in the name of defining reasonable precautions, require a quite inefficient level of staffing—might, that is, misperceive the cost of taking precautions compared to the cost of letting an occasional "emergency" requiring overtime take place. If we assume that workers' pay bears a relation to the efficiency of the firm, this proposed law, as applied, might not even be good for workers themselves.

On the other hand, it is also true that the current pattern of the law—letting management require overtime as it will—appears to undervalue certain of the costs involved: specifically, the disruption of other-than-work relationships and rhythms. For these costs of requiring overtime, the workers are probably the better judges; certainly they have more knowledge of their particular web of relationships.

The upshot is that, once we are past what everyone would agree to be emergency situations, there is probably no one—manager, worker, or judge—in a position to assess properly all the implications of requiring, or refusing, overtime work. Thus it is perhaps not surprising that the state legislatures have refused to move from the status quo. The sole statute currently in force, in the state of Maine, stipulates only that employers cannot require workers to work more than 80 hours of *overtime* in any two-week period[55]—an almost laughably trivial legal protection were it not for the fact that there were indeed some employers in Maine who had exceeded that limit.[56] (For that matter, even the much more limited Family and Medical Leave Act was not easy to pass; it was, indeed, vetoed by the first President Bush, and his veto was sustained by Congress. Only after President Clinton was elected was the FMLA signed into law.)[57]

Nevertheless, there is considerable reason to believe that the legislatures are making a mistake—reason to believe, that is, that the best alternative to the current situation would be a thoughtfully drafted statute empowering workers to make the final choice whether to accept overtime or not. As we have seen, it is unlikely that the employment relationship as a whole is going to be reconstituted any time soon by giving workers general protection against being fired except for cause. Assuming at-will employment, if we give particular rights to workers, the risk is more that the rights will prove to be of little use than that they will be abused. For when particular rights are established in what are otherwise relationships subject to market mechanisms and private sources of power, there is always the danger that these other forces will overwhelm the law's effects. This is especially true when the right conferred is not a specified entitlement but rather the power to make a voluntary choice, for who knows what influences can be brought to bear before a "voluntary" choice is made? Even a legal guarantee that rights can be invoked without retribution may not protect against—or may not be thought to protect against—the many subtle realities of the real-life workplace. There is, for example, evidence to suggest that, quite apart from the problem of the economics of unpaid leave, workers are hesitant to assert their rights under the FMLA; employees are afraid that if they take leave, others—co-workers as well as managers—will perceive them to be slackers.[58] We could reasonably expect similar workplace pressures to temper any inclination on the part of workers to use a right to refuse overtime in willful disregard of the practical situation. In short, it is reasonable to think that giving the choice to the worker rather than the manager—that is, to the party who, because he is generally less powerful, must listen harder to the other party—will result in fewer errors overall.[59]

This question of how effective new rights would be, conditions the analysis of a great many other possible proposals for managing the boundaries of work time. In situations where a new rule would do away with some of the existing protections for organized time, there is reason to be skeptical about whether the gain would be worth the loss.

In the last several Congresses, bills have been introduced for statutes to be called variously the "Working Families Flexibility Act," the "Family Friendly Workplace Act," or the "Workplace Flexibility Act."[60] Two of the proposals contained in these bills—called "comptime" and "biweekly work programs"—deserve special note.

In 1985, the Fair Labor Standards Act was amended to allow state and local governments to enter contracts with their employees providing "in lieu of overtime compensation, compensatory time off at a rate not less than one and one-half hours for each hour of employment for which overtime compensation is required."[61] The pending "comptime" proposal aims to make a similar rule applicable to private employment.

Comptime was given very serious consideration in 1997; it passed the House of Representatives but died in the Senate. As reported by the House Committee on Education and the Workforce,[62] the bill provided for comptime either as part of a collective bargaining agreement or as a separate arrangement specifically agreed to by an employer and individual employees. Up to 240 hours (that is, compensation at time-and-a-half for 160 hours of overtime work) could be "banked" by the employee. This banked time could then be used to get time off without losing pay. The bill provided that, after having made a request, the employee "shall be permitted by the employee's employer to use such time within a reasonable period after making the request if the use of the compensatory time does not unduly disrupt the operations of the employer."[63] The bill also stipulated that an employer would violate the law if it threatened or coerced employees either to accept comptime instead of overtime payment or to use their comptime.[64] Finally, there were various provisions for cashing out unused banked time at the regular hourly rate (that is, at time-and-a-half for the underlying overtime work).

The favorable House Committee Report[65] emphasized the value of the bill for families. Comptime, it said, would make room for irregularly arising family responsibilities that employees would otherwise have to meet, if at all, with unpaid leave or vacation time; and comptime would allow for a needed flexibility across the barrier of the 40-hour week erected by the FLSA. The Committee also pointed out that public employers and employees already had the freedom to make such arrangements. As for the possibility of employer coercion leading to unwanted loss of overtime pay, the provisions in the bill specifically prohibiting coercion, plus the indirect power given to employees by their ability to have their time cashed out, were sufficient, in the Committee's view, to meet this fear of abuse.

The dissenting minority stressed instead its assessment that employees would in fact have neither the freedom to choose or refuse comptime, nor the power to decide when to use what comptime they had. "In the real world, many employees are reluctant or fearful to buck their employer's wishes regarding their terms and conditions of employment."[66] Public-sector employees, generally organized and in a less pressured environment, were a different case. The net result of the bill, said the dissenters, would be longer hours at less pay.

The Committee Report in the Senate helped make the case for comptime as family-friendly by quoting a mother with two children who testified as follows:

> [Overtime] pay is important to me. However, the time with my family is more important. If I had a choice there are times when I would prefer to take comp time in lieu of overtime. What makes this idea appealing is that I would be able to choose which option best suits my situation.
>
> Just recently, my son was ill and I had to stay at home with him. I took a day of vacation which I would have preferred to use for vacation. I did not want to take unpaid leave. . . . If I had had the choice, I would have used comp time in lieu of overtime for that day off from work. Besides, I would have only had to use about five and one-half hours of comp time to cover that 8 hour day.[67]

But these supposed family-friendly advantages of comptime are in fact based on an optical illusion. It may look as if the employee is getting 8 hours off for roughly 5½ hours of work, but in reality she is getting 8 hours off in exchange for the roughly 8 hours of pay that she would get for working 5½ hours of overtime. Working overtime, getting paid for it, and then taking a day of unpaid leave, comes to the very same thing as comptime. Thus, the real crux of the matter is not how the employee "pays" for a day's leave, but who decides whether and when leave is available in the first place.

The proposed statutory standard (which tracks the law currently applicable to government employees) foresees the employee making a request to use comptime and then being permitted within a reasonable time to use it if that does not "unduly disrupt" the employer's operations. Leaving aside the point that a relatively formal application process does not seem well-tailored to emergency situations like a child's sickness, this standard gives the employer considerable room to object to any particular proposed time. If the employer is able to channel the use of comptime into periods when work is, in any case, slow— if, that is, the employer does not have to pay other workers overtime (or hire temporary substitutes) to cover for those taking leave—then there will be a net saving to the employer as a result of its ability to substitute this slow time for otherwise-due overtime wages. Of course an employer can, under the current system, redirect requests for unpaid leave, too. But the fact remains that the employer's and employee's interests may well be opposed and that the enunciated legal standard may not be sufficient to empower the employee. In an article analyzing these comptime proposals, one economist sized up the situation in this way:

> On the high road, the employer grants the comp time option to all those who request it, lets employees use it when they need it, applies no pressure regarding the selection or use of comp time and dutifully cashes out comp time credits upon request. In contrast, on the "low road," overtime

hours are shifted toward workers choosing the comp time option and pressure is applied both to select the comp time option and to use it only when output demand slows.[68]

An even gloomier conclusion was reached by another analyst who, after a thorough examination, concluded that comptime, by making overtime cheaper for the employer, would probably increase the use of overtime; and that it would, by its very complexity, make it harder to enforce the underlying provisions of the basic overtime law, the Fair Labor Standards Act.[69]

The biggest cost of the comptime proposal, however, is the possibility that its adoption would help undermine the week as the basic unit of work time.[70] This danger is even more clearly present in the other nostrum proposed in this set of Congressional bills, the possibility that employers and employees could voluntarily agree to establish "Biweekly Work Programs."[71] Under this plan, the basic unit of work would be 80 hours over two weeks. Overtime (which would be compensated in money, not comptime) would not accrue until after that limit had been reached, unless it was sudden and unpredicted overtime. Thus, workers could be scheduled to work for more than 40 hours in one week, without crediting of time-and-a-half wages, if they correspondingly worked for fewer than 40 work hours in the other week of the pair. For instance, employees could work 48 hours in one week and 32 in the next, getting an extra "day off," without the employer paying more than straight-time wages.

As we saw in Chapter 4, there has been a considerable use in recent years of "flextime," in which, in its most common form, the employee still works 8 hours a day, five days a week, but has control over when to start the work day, when to finish, and perhaps when to have lunch; and the somewhat less common use of the "compressed work week," in which the employee works four 10-hour days. The "Biweekly Work Programs" scheme essentially recapitulates these forms, but puts them on a two-week basis. It proposes, in effect, a trade: greater choice but a less forceful structural norm. Flextime and the compressed work week occurring within the individual week do not pose this alternative, since the structural norm of the FLSA is the week itself. Any increase in employees' power to determine their hours of work within a single week costs workers, at least in terms of their legal rights, nothing: it simply transfers to them some of the power that the background legal norms give to their employers. But this new biweekly proposal *would* cost employees something: the norm of the week as the basic unit in which work time is figured.

Is this a worthwhile trade? In the abstract, real costs inhere in the fact that the FLSA's norm—the week of 40 hours with overtime beyond that—is mandatory. This requirement necessarily means that sometimes both parties, employer and employee, will genuinely want to do something that will be against the law. The law both denies their joint freedom and, if they were making rational choices, reduces their joint welfare. The proposed legislation tries to make use of this theory by promising that no worker has to operate on a biweekly basis unless he (or his union) agrees to do so. Biweekly programs are to be allowed only pursuant to a collective bargaining agreement, or to a specific agreement between employer and employee "if the agreement or understanding was entered into knowingly and voluntarily by such employee and was not a condition of employment."[72]

In context, however, with biweekly programs just as with comptime proposals, we can imagine a high road and a low road. On the high road, biweekly work schedules would be an option made available by employers to employees to choose, or not, as they like, and would enable those employees for whom an extra day off is especially valuable to have that day predictably and without loss of pay. On the low road, employers for their own reasons could invent work schedules that are even less synchronized with family responsibilities than at present—for example, ten days "on" followed by four days "off"—and pressure employees into signing the necessary documents. Which road is more likely to be followed depends in part on the balance of power between workers and employers. It also depends on whether the legal prohibition on making an employee's agreement to a biweekly schedule a condition of employment is effective. We are, in short, back to the problem of how to empower workers effectively in the context of an overall relationship that is so dependent on market forces.

The week is a fundamental—indeed probably the most important—structure of time in our society. School time ticks on a weekday-versus-weekend basis. Religious observances have a weekly rhythm. Social and recreational events, even TV programs (or at least first-run TV programs), recur every seven days. For a great many people—those who have to synchronize their lives with others—the loss of the week as the fundamental unit of work time would be a very great loss. Flextime within the week respects these rhythms; flextime outside of the individual week— the "biweekly work program"—very well may not. For most people, the risks involved in accepting the proposed trade are greater than the likely rewards.

We live in a society in which, for a variety of reasons, the demands of the workplace threaten to destroy the balance of life. Many of the efforts to preserve the needed balance, or to restore it where it has been lost, rely on notions of flexibility, so that family or civic or personal needs can be "fit in." "Fit in" to what? To the rhythm of work. A push for flexibility concedes the dominance of the workplace at the same time that it tries to deal with it. By contrast, the basic norm of the 40-hour week sets a boundary to work so that other rhythms have a chance to establish themselves on their own terms. In the end, control over the basic work week is a necessary starting point. Professionals who are "exempt" from the FLSA have a great deal of trouble putting bounds on their work time; the fact that they also often have great flexibility in scheduling their work is not a satisfactory substitute for having the basic limit. It is only within the framework set by a basic norm, such as the 40-hour week, that ideas of flexibility are correctly viewed as providing needed "wiggle room" rather than representing capitulation to the dominant social forces.

7

The General Case

In the course of this book we have examined a variety of questions regarding how we, as a society, should structure our time. The preceding chapters have investigated these questions in a number of specific settings, including the way the law establishes how we tell time, the legal restrictions on selling and working on Sunday, the development of the 40-hour work week and its legal protection through the Fair Labor Standards Act, mandatory school attendance laws, and the legal mechanisms that address conflicts at the boundaries of work time and family time. In each of these discussions, we considered the issues contextually, focusing on the facts and arguments that were especially pertinent to the specific situation; this, of course, was necessary if we were to evaluate practical policies. Along the way, we also gained an appreciation for the many legal techniques that can be used to help structure social time, and for the power of looking at issues in terms of all four facets of social time: allocation, coordination, rhythm, and texture.

But in treating the matter in such a fashion, we also took a stance or viewpoint—a way of thinking about the value of structures in society, and of balance in individual lives—that was assumed rather than defended. To complete our consideration of the law of time, it is thus necessary to step back from particular contexts and consider more theoretically the general case: when, how, and to what extent should the law provide a structure for social time?

We can frame the analysis of this broad question by imagining two alternative legal regimes: a "freedom of time" regime and a "constructed time" regime. The basic concept underlying a "freedom of time" legal regime is that the law should provide a set of rules and processes that facilitate the efforts of individuals and institutions—non-governmental entities—in making their own particular arrangements regarding time, but not go further. Carrying this out would involve four legal mechanisms. First, the law would establish (or officially support) a general social order that would allow parties to speak a "common language" in their dealings. Thus, for example, the existing Uniform Time Act could well be part of a freedom of time regime. Second, it would enforce the understandings regarding time that individuals and institutions reached. In legal terms, this would mostly involve enforcing the parties' contracts, taking "contract" not in the narrow sense of a signed, formal document but in the broad sense of any voluntary private agreement. Third, the law would provide background or "default" rules to fill out the parties' agreements when they were not sufficiently specific. These would be rules like those we have examined involving workers' obligations at the beginning and end of the work day, so long as they were constructed to facilitate further bargaining rather than to predetermine a desired result. And fourth, to protect the freedom of the parties, the law would have to police the forces that could be brought to bear on them. This would involve establishing both a law of duress (so that workers could not be made to work 60 or 80 hours a week at gunpoint) and a law against discrimination (so that others could not exact reprisals against those who, for example, agreed to work on Sundays).

By contrast, the basic idea behind a "constructed time" regime is that the law should create mechanisms at the societal level specifically designed to further the various purposes of social time. Several different mechanisms are available. The archetype of the approach is the regime of the Blue Laws, which separated the realm of time into six-sevenths commercial time and one-seventh noncommercial (family, religious, or social) time, specifically on some view (religious or secular) of what constituted a balanced life. But the Fair Labor Standards Act, at least as applied in current circumstances, has a lot of construction in it, too. The modern purpose of setting 40 hours as the presumptive limit of the work week is to make sure that there is time for other activities, and to make sure that that time is available on a recurrent, rhythmic basis. The fact that the limit can be exceeded by paying time-and-a-half—that the law sets a price rather than announcing a flat prohibition—makes the rule less constraining, but does not deny the fundamental social policy involved. (If one could bargain out of the Act without paying the premium, it would be more like the default rules of the freedom of time regime; but the law does not allow that.) Finally, even the way government runs its own functions can be seen as part of the constructed time regime, if they are purposefully arranged for their broader social impact. If, for example, mail is not delivered on Sunday not because of lack of demand, but specifically to further the noncommercial nature of the day—and historically that was the case[1]—then even the pattern of mail delivery is part of the official construction of time.

Needless to say, history does not present us with a pure case of either of these hypothetical patterns. But if we were to judge by predominant tendencies, we probably would say (in light of the history we have already looked at) that as of the mid-twentieth century, America had established a version of a constructed time regime. Venerable Sunday closing and holiday-protective laws were still in force in most of the country; at least since the 1920s a mandatory school year of substantial proportions and definite contours had been established virtually everywhere; and since the late 1930s the 40-hour week was national law for many workers, and state law for yet others.

Developments in the intervening half-century have been mixed. On the side of greater social construction, the 40-hour week has been gradually extended to even more employees, and the Family and Medical Leave Act has been passed; on the side of greater individuation, Sunday closing has been gradually eliminated in most of the country, holidays have been liberalized, and legislation needed to make flextime possible has been passed. Looking to the future, proposals to enlarge workers' rights by extending the FMLA are part of the political agenda; so too are proposals to make both the work week and the school year more flexible. As we begin the twenty-first century, then, our society seems to be uncertain as to which path to follow.

This mixed picture mirrors our more general social uncertainty regarding economic and social "regulation." Over the last few decades we have seen an increase of legal regulation in some quarters—such as control over air and water pollution and workplace safety—side by side with a decrease in others—such as deregulation of the airline, telecommunications, and financial services industries. So another way of stating the question of the general case is, should we "deregulate" time as we have many other things, regulate it anew as we have done with yet other things, or pretty much stand pat?

It is a mistake—but one that is often made—to see the choice between regulation and deregulation as equivalent to that between the presence and absence of law. Even the most laissez-faire of economic systems assumed a considerable legal structure that prevented violence, protected private property, and enforced contracts. Similarly, the decision to allow individuals and non-governmental institutions to do most temporal structuring—if we made a decision in favor of a "freedom of time" regime—would rely heavily on the law. Although less immediately visible, the law of duress preventing the use of force to extract long working hours is as much law as the law of required school attendance. In the freedom of time regime, the law would be involved in establishing the negotiating positions of the various private parties—for example, by stipulating what the default rules would be—and in enforcing the outcomes of private ordering—for instance, by providing remedies for breach of contract. A statute mandating a 40-hour work week, a collective bargaining agreement stipulating a 40-hour work week, and an individual contract providing for a 40-hour work week are all legal artifacts, shaped from their inception by legal norms and enforceable through legal institutions. The fundamental choice, then, is between two different forms of the law of time, both of them very legal.

Clearly a freedom of time regime would rely heavily on the workings of the market, and so we may start our consideration of these alternatives by asking how the usual reasons in favor of relying on the market apply to time. That argument might look like this: Time is an essential resource to be allocated among tasks to be accomplished.[2] When time is viewed as a resource to be allocated, time structures—especially those that cannot be varied by the parties, or varied only with difficulty—appear to be irrational. They set up barriers to achieving the most efficient solution. If, for example, a society forbade all night work, that would prevent firms from doing at night things which are best segregated from the work of the day; the very fact that without the prohibition there would be night work serves as proof (in this framework of thought) that there is such work worth doing. It is better, in this view, to let the market decide what time is most valuable, and by how much. An uncoerced contract between private parties both exemplifies their freedom and increases their joint welfare; a system of such contracts—the free market—maximizes the overall satisfaction of preferences.[3]

The standard critique of these broad claims on behalf of a system of free contract is that private arrangements are neither so free nor so welfare-maximizing as is supposed. For example, in response to the freedom of time proposition that the trade-off between working additional hours for further rewards, and spending those same hours at leisure, is best left to the market, it will be said that what the law takes to be "free" are circumstances that from other points of view are quite coercive. This is true of, perhaps even especially true of, circumstances of vigorous and open competition. Thus, many workers not protected by the Fair Labor Standards Act are of the view that labor markets today are very competitive and, for just that reason, workers have to be willing to work long hours—or someone else will. The response to this critique will be that workers who do not want to work so many hours can make themselves more attractive by offering to work for less money; that even though individual workers' choices will be constrained by competitive forces, the market, by equilibrating various workers' different desires for material goods and for leisure, will generate the greatest overall satisfaction of these desires that is possible. Lobbing the ball over the net once more, the critic will then point to structural features of the situation that prevent the market from working in this idealized fashion. Thus, Juliet Schor argues that for various institutional reasons—for instance, because firms like having control over employees, and have more control over those who spend more of their lives at work—firms prefer to employ a smaller set of workers willing to work long hours over a larger, equally productive, perhaps (on the logic of her argument) even somewhat lower-priced set of workers, each working shorter hours.[4]

If critiques of this sort are true, then properly drafted legislation setting limits on private arrangements could improve the performance of the market. Since such legislation inherently would be taking a position on what the desirable contours of work time are, its passage would constitute movement toward a constructed time regime.

But debates such as these—whichever side has the better of them—do not get to the central issues regarding the desirability, or not, of the freedom of time regime. This is so because thus far the question of social time has been treated as if it were a problem with only a single dimension: What should be the number of hours of work, what the number of hours of leisure? In principle, both sides have agreed that this is a question of proper allocation, perhaps even ideally of efficient allocation, given the individual desires of the contracting parties; they have only differed on whether the market is accurately registering the necessary information.

But time, as we know, has many facets. It is not only a resource; it is not just like money. As we have seen throughout this book, in addition to thinking about the number of hours spent at work, say, or at school, we must think of the pattern those hours form, of the way one person's hours relate to another's, of the resulting texture of life. Any adequate theory of what the law of time should look like must address its multifaceted nature and not treat the problem as equivalent to finding the most efficient mix of uses of a fungible commodity. Thus it is necessary to restart our analysis with a further description of what it is we are trying to achieve.

People live socially. They must do more than allocate their time to activities; the activities to which they devote their time must be synchronized, or if not synchronized then ordered

chronologically. Unless they are to live by a new chronological order every day, their activities must be rhythmic as well. This is
true of economically productive activities and also—perhaps historically even more so—true of civic and expressive activities.

A modern society such as ours—a market society, a mass society, a liberal democratic society—presents this general phenomenon in a new form. The successful functioning of a modern
society requires not only a more careful allocation of time, but
also a more articulated and forceful structure of time. True, the
rationality of modern economic life is (as Max Weber showed
long ago)[5] based on the parsimonious control of time as well as
money; but it is also true that production which has been more
intensely socialized requires greater temporal organization to be
successful. Large numbers of people in individual workplaces,
and large numbers of different workplaces, must be closely linked
in temporal proximity. The events of cultural life and civic life,
too, coordinate more people and need to be more tightly scheduled. For most young people, schooling also takes place in an institutional setting, with its concomitant demand for a temporal
framework. Yes, the amount of time that activities take in this society is carefully measured; but yes also, things happen at a set
time, often a time repeated on a rhythmic basis. Indeed, as all the
adults in more and more families work outside the home, even
family time takes on a rationalized and organized aspect. Because
of the rationalization and institutional development of modern
society, work is separated from home; both are separated from
school; we have various religious, social, and professional groups;
and all of these are something different from the overarching political society. Each of these institutional separations is marked, to
a greater or lesser extent, by a differentiation of the organization
and texture of time.

This multiplicity of institutional settings and group affiliations
has implications far beyond getting the society's work done, al-

though that is, of course, important. This pattern also sets the basis for the freedom and fluidity of liberal democratic society. We often lose sight of this because we use a language of liberty that makes freedom seem highly individualistic, that makes the proposition that people work and live in groups sound inherently illiberal. But we are not speaking of ascriptive groups, into which people are born and from which they cannot leave. The ability to exit is here, as elsewhere, the fundamental social embodiment of freedom seen as a negative right.[6] On the more positive side, it is institutions that are intermediate between the individual and the whole society—especially families and religious groups—that give people the social support they need to develop as individuated and independent actors. More broadly yet, it is within cooperative groups—and here we might especially point to social and civic groups—that we act, and learn to act, in the participatory, democratic fashion that typifies political freedom as Americans understand it.[7] And still more grandly, the maintenance of a welter of differentiated but overlapping groups and institutions, performing disparate tasks throughout the society, is the best protection against, virtually the antithesis of, the totalitarian regimes that represent the darkest possibility of modern life.

This differentiation of institutional life also has important implications for how individuals ought best to live their lives. The typical individual in our type of society plays several roles in several different social environments. This is not a fact of nature. Societies may inherently have many tasks to perform, but they can be done in a continuous social setting, with work, family life, religion, and politics all being carried out by a single group living in a single place; this is the pattern of many traditional communities and of some modern communal experiments as well. To make this communal approach the dominant pattern for a modern society would, however, require an enormous restructuring. In any case—perhaps because our sensibilities have been shaped by the more differentiated modern world—this pattern seems too confining to most of us to be our ideal. Even the more limited conjunction of work and child-rearing represented by working at home with children at home seems attractive to some of us but clearly not to all.

Given that our society places the individual into several roles in several separated institutional settings, the appropriate ideal for the life of each individual is the ideal of balance. Human beings will live more fulfilling lives if they participate, substantially and with personal commitment, in several of the activities and several of the settings in which they must live. This may sound platitudinous, but in fact it is a contestable concept. Some might think— some do think—that the most fulfilling lives are led by those who completely lose themselves in one activity—artistic, political, religious, or familial. And indeed there is something to be said for this alternative ideal of coherence: it avoids the stress, some might say the alienation, of separating the meaning of one's life into distinct (and potentially competing) parcels. Whether a whole society could be composed of people who live this way is not at all clear—for, after all, even great artists or fervent revolutionaries must live in a world in which mundane activities go on. But possible or not, the simple truth is that pursuing a single commitment to the exclusion of all else, whatever its virtues, is too heroic for most of us. Given the kind of society in which we live and the kinds of desires and abilities we have, for most of us some mix of working in a workplace, being with and contributing to family at home, participating in religious or civic activities with a group of like-minded acquaintances, getting together with another group for sports or a hobby, and having some time "to ourselves"—or at least most of these—represents the most desirable life. In short, balance is our ideal.

If these last few paragraphs fairly describe our condition, which legal regime for time—the freedom of time regime or the constructed time regime—better fits our situation? The case for having a constructed time regime is based on the claim that strong structures of time vitally support our need as a society to maintain a healthy plurality of differentiated institutions, and our need as individuals to maintain a healthy balance among our commitments to the various institutions in which we participate. This is so, the argument continues, because the ways in which we use time are not merely by-products of social life; they help constitute social life.

It is perhaps a commonplace to say that the sharing of values, through the common devotion of time to them, produces social cohesion. Holidays, when they serve their intended purpose, proclaim the existence of widely held social values, and by doing so serve not only to express, but also to create and perpetuate, the solidarity of the group: of the religion, or, if a public holiday, of the society as a whole.

What is less often realized, but practically speaking of far greater importance, is that the use of time structures to coordinate activities and to give them rhythm—even without the creation of specially meaningful or textured time—also creates social solidarity. Strong groups thrive on activities that are done together, or if not simultaneously, then in purposeful sequence. True, one can speak of a group in which each individual does things on his or her own time. One can say that all those who subscribe to a particular magazine, or contribute money to a specific cause, are a "group"; or that all those who submit their comments to an on-line bulletin board constitute a "chat group." But there is not much cohesion in groups such as these. By contrast, the very act of purposefully coordinating one's time with the time of others affirmatively creates group feeling; the very habit of doing things with reference to what other members of the group are doing creates solidarity. One need go no further than understanding the value to families of doing things together to see the truth of this idea. The structure of time is more than just a facilitating circumstance; it helps establish the group.

The point is even stronger when activities are not only coordinated, but also given a rhythm. When many people act in rhythm—when they jointly participate in an activity according to a repeated time pattern—they tend to form into a yet more tightly knit social group. The historian William McNeill has recently speculated on the existence of an innate bonding mechanism among humans who dance, drill, or work together in proximity according to a rhythm.[8] Whatever the mechanism, anthropologists and sociologists have long commented on the importance of social rhythms—for example, the recurrence of ordinary activities according to the "week" as constructed by a specific society—in helping to constitute particular ways of life and groups' consciousness of their own distinctiveness. Solidaristic groups have a rhythm, in part because solidarity creates a rhythm, but also because a rhythm creates solidarity.[9]

These mechanisms operate not only at the level of the whole society, but also with regard to the groups and institutional structures within the society. A pervasive case is provided by the ordinary workplace. Work time is, for a great many people, both highly coordinated and very rhythmic; it presents emphatic and repeating time patterns. The strong sense people have of needing to be at work at their "usual" time to participate in the group's activities and to play their roles in it—the way in which, as Arlie Hochschild reports in The Time Bind,[10] people want to spend time at work—reflects in part this time-structured solidarity. So (by contrast) does the sense of anomie common among retirees who suddenly lose their daily rhythm.

Of the kinds of time we have examined in this book, work time and school time are strongly structured, coordinating closely a great deal of activity and giving it a strong rhythm. Much weaker are the time structures that enhance the cohesion of other types of groups. The framework of family time is of special concern. To say that the issue is that not enough time is allotted to the family is too flimsy. It is rather that families lack control of the structure of their time. The rhythm of the family is very often not its own rhythm: dinner at a recurrent time, family get-togethers for recreation at a recurrent time, TV watching as a group at a recurrent time—but at best the shadow of other rhythms: dinner when we all get home from work or school. And all too often even the basic element of coordination—we will all have dinner at the same time—is very hard to achieve. To dismiss this as merely a sign of the weakening of the family is a mistake. It is a contributing cause.

Much the same might be said regarding the declining cohesion of the community and social groups so important to our civic and political life. Disparate and disjoint activities—such as writing a check to contribute—are no substitute for meeting together and doing together, which are increasingly hard to arrange in a society that lacks reliable, rhythmic "open" time.[11] "From the point of view of social connectedness," as Robert Putnam has written, "the Environmental Defense Fund and a bowling league are just not in the same category."[12] The failure to have additional strong time structures thus threatens the existence of the vast panoply of intermediate groups that give our social and political life its distinctive cast.

Our time structures that only weakly protect activities other than work or school also threaten the ability of individuals to achieve balance in their own lives. Balance represents an ideal of playing the several roles one is called upon, or wants, to play, in a satisfying combination; and to play a role in modern society, one must ordinarily play it with reference to a group. If one cannot coordinate with the group, cannot enter into a rhythm with the group, the role itself will be impoverished. But the point goes further, because the way in which society structures time also helps establish the system of normative claims upon which the ideal of balance depends. What, for example, is the force of the claim: "I can't do that, I have to be home for dinner"? Is it as strong as "I can't do that, I have to be at work," or as "I can't do that, I have to be at school"? In large parts of our society, the comparative force of the first claim has decreased in recent years. People do not think that family time is as coordinated, as rhythmic—and therefore as compulsory for the individual—as work time or school time. But if the general view is that family time is secondary, then it will be harder to negotiate the intricacies of life to achieve a balance of one's use of time.

What, then, is the desirable shape of social time? Our structure for time should support an appropriate allocation of human time among the various functions of the society. It should support the maintenance of numerous types of institutions and groups within the society. And it should support the individual's ability to balance the demands of multiple social roles. This structure will not exist, says the proponent of constructed time, unless we purposefully and forcefully construct it; what we need is not only to continue maintaining the structure we have, but indeed to create additional structural elements that will help rebalance those forms of social time—family and civic—that are now getting short shrift.

It is possible to respond to this line of argument by saying that any attention to matters other than the efficient allocation of time is bad, because it will result in less than the maximum possible production of goods and services in light of the competing demands for leisure. Even if the factual predicate is true—and we have already seen that it will not be so easy to know how to arrange for that hypothetical maximum—such a deification of the Gross National Product does not seem very sensible given the importance of the individual and social issues at stake.

Much more serious are the arguments that contend that, even

considering all the implications of the structure of social time—
the need to preserve a profusion of institutions and also to provide
balance to individual lives—the constructed time regime has serious flaws. There are, indeed, at least three strong objections: that
a constructed time regime does not very effectively produce
the supposed outcome; that it is too constraining to individual
choice; and that it prevents much-needed social experimentation.
Although the stereotypical proponents of these arguments—
respectively the economist, the libertarian, and the postmodern
cultural critic—may seem very different from one another, these
contentions are in large part mutually reinforcing.

To begin, even when the many facets of time and the numerous
social goals to be achieved are considered, there is a real efficiency
problem with the constructed time regime: whatever rules the law
adopts may not produce the desired outcomes very cleanly. For
within each of the abstract categories that seem to encompass
most of the society's time demands—work time, school time, family time, and so forth—lies a concrete differentiation of life which
seems to resist a tight temporal structure. One form of production
calls for around-the-clock tending of machinery; another does not.
One business wants to be tightly coordinated with events on the
other side of the globe; another couldn't care less. Many families
have children and need to be mindful of school time; many do not.
Cultural life for some people revolves around events that grab the
attention of a large audience at a particular time, like spectator
sports; for others it does not. Even religious observance, often
highly synchronized for any one group of believers, is highly diverse for the population considered as a whole. This does not
mean that there should be no rhythms that extend across the
whole society; one important group of which we are members is
the society itself. Rituals, such as public holidays, that remind us
of that fact—and, indeed, help create that fact—have their place.
But we cannot assume that the rhythms of other sorts of groups

and institutions in the society fall into a single pattern for each category. If we try to establish a constructed time regime, we will always be bedeviled by the question of "fit": given the range of social life, any broad pattern will necessarily be overly broad. By contrast, say those more in favor of freedom of time, the smaller-scale arrangements that people make for themselves are likely to mesh with their particular circumstances much more closely.

Given this profusion of ways of living and doing, constructed time structures can also be seen as representing the unwarranted imposition of choice by some on others. Why should the law take sides as to whose desires are satisfied? If a society forbade all working at night, that might enable those who want to work during the day to have peace and quiet, or family get-togethers, at night—but what about those others who see the night as the last frontier, and want to do their work as loners?[13] If their desires match the needs of a prospective employer, why should the objections of others be given preference by the law? The exercise of choice by non-governmental entities, rather than by government, has always constituted a large part of what Americans have considered freedom to be. Since some of the choices to be made surely represent not only personal, but cultural preferences as well, allowing individuals to choose would also further the goal of evenhandedness in regard to the many subgroups that make up modern America.

But the question of diversity goes further than multiplicity in this subgroup sense. It also has to do with the development of new patterns of living to match the new world of time and space compression brought on by new technologies and a new global connectedness.[14] A system of constructed time, if it does not simply favor the interests of the politically powerful, will favor the circumstances of the modal members of society, those who lie near the center of the statistician's bell curve. But, say the critics, the future of the society—like the future of Darwin's species—

lies with the eccentric or mutant forms of social life, which today are at the edge of the distribution but tomorrow will be found to have been fitter to survive. Creativity, the argument continues, depends on the contextual knowledge of individuals or very small groups. Just as more vital forms of urban life grow up in helter-skelter cities than in the planned one-way-of-life high-rises of modern architects, so too will better forms of the use of time thrive in a regime of freedom of time.

All of these possible arguments against a constructed time regime can be seen in the case that was in fact made against Sunday closing laws. If shopkeepers and shoppers were both willing to trade, it was abrasive to tell them they could not. Specifying Sunday as the day for noncommercial activities illegitimately reinforced the cultural hegemony of certain religions. Adapting to new uses of leisure was better done bit by bit throughout the society, rather than in the name of a single vision of the good life. Citizens could decide better than the government whether in their particular circumstances it was worth more to them to go shopping, or not, on their days off from work. So, the critics would say, just as Sunday closing laws now look like an anachronistic holdover from another social era, so too do tightly constructed laws regarding work, schooling, and the like look more like the America of the 1950s, with its quest for homogeneity and planned progress, than the America in which we now live.

There is no doubt that these arguments have force. To evaluate just how strong they are, however, we need to ask comparable questions about the freedom-of-time alternative. Can the desirable multifocal arrangement of individuals and institutions be established purely on the basis of private bilateral agreements supported legally by a freedom-of-time regime?

Let us start with the individual. He (or she) wants to work at a reasonably remunerative job, and also wants to feel that he is part of a workplace. He wants to eat dinner or watch TV with his family. He wants to go to a place of worship and pray with the other members of his congregation. He wants to participate in a charitable organization or be part of a political movement. He wants to relax with a group of his friends. He wants some time by himself. Each of these wants, except perhaps the last (and in many circumstances even including the last), can be satisfied only if he can coordinate his actions with others—and, in our society, usually with a different set of others for each of the activities.

Now let us suppose that the individual tries to arrange this situation purely through a process of agreement. How does he formulate his negotiating position for any of the deals he will have to make? Since he is interested not only in the allocation of time, but in coordination with others and the rhythm of their groups, it seems that he needs to know, in order to make any single arrangement, the outcome (or at least the likely outcome) of a great many other arrangements. For example, he wants to eat dinner with his family, and is willing to negotiate with his employer, and even give up something in wages, in order to make this happen. But when is dinner? It is (by hypothesis) at the time agreed upon by the members of the family. To reach that agreement, all the other members of the family have to think about what else they need to fit into their schedules (team sports? another job? school?) before they can agree on a dinner time. But if we are working purely by agreement, going to school (for example) could take place on any day of the week, any time of the day, for any length of time. Going to school is itself a group activity, so determining when the children will go to school will require negotiation with numerous others. And so on. The complexity is astonishing. Arranging social time solely by private agreement turns out to be a very radical proposition.

The same complexities can be seen from the institutional point of view. Anyone who has tried to get ten people together at the same time and place for a meeting—simply as a matter of personal agreement and in the absence of a pre-existing rule that stipulates a certain time for meetings—knows how complex a task that is. How, acting solely by private agreement, would we ever get even a hundred people together at the same time and place to pray, each of whom had to work (or go to school) with a hundred other people at another time and place, and each of whom had a few family members with whom they wanted to eat, let us say once a day, at yet another time and place? Once again, the arrangement to be achieved requires a highly complicated interweaving of people and institutions.[15]

What, then, would happen in this situation? Since we are dealing with a hypothetical universe, we cannot be sure. But it seems likely that the institutions and groups with the power to do so would insist that their time needs and rhythms be attended to first. For their part, individuals would deal first with the most powerful institution they had to deal with, or perhaps with the one they cared the most about, and then would try to make the best of what remained. For most people, the outcome would probably be that they would anchor their time according to the demands of their workplaces (or if young, according to their parents' time, which would mean their parents' workplaces), although some might put family, church, school, or civic activity first. The net effect would be that work time (whatever that time itself looked like) would be the basic clock of society. The other activities of society would operate on residual time. Negotiated agreements between individuals and social institutions would not suffice to produce anything like the balance we desire. Seen from this angle, the existing laws which further a constructed time regime, far from representing an anachronistic social order, in fact incorporate vital protections for the weaker institutions of society against a work time that would be even more predominant without them than it is today.

But, the proponent of freedom of time might respond, this

mental experiment is not a fair test of the freedom of time regime. While it is inherent in the regime that the government not provide a mandatory structure for time, it is not necessarily the case that the only elements in the system would be background legal rules and private agreements. The people making these agreements would still live in a society. Of course they would need norms of some sort to guide their plans and actions; without some sort of structure, the large number of decisions that would have to be made would become unmanageable. However, informal social norms—or more precisely, norms that are not legally established—could reduce alternatives to a manageable number and facilitate predictions of what others would be trying to arrange. These norms could provide all the structure that is needed without being rigidified, as the law inevitably is.

For this conception to work in practice, however, merely the existence of some social norms regarding time is not sufficient. The norms must aim at the sort of institutional and personal balance we are looking for, and they must be effective. Now, norms without an institutional locus tend not to have staying power or force; a mere abstract social commitment to balance will not be enough. However, since we are dealing with the boundaries between institutions—having removed by hypothesis the general force of government and specifically structured law—no individual institution will have a structural commitment to balance. So the practical issue is whether each set of institutions will generate a powerful enough normative structure to anchor its claims vis-à-vis other institutions. In other words, the issue is whether the scenario just sketched, of the most powerful institutions getting their own way with time, would be borne out, or whether, instead, there would be a balance among countervailing institutions sufficient to create (or to allow individuals to create) a balance of social time.

This is not an easy question to answer. Undoubtedly some institutions—notably churches—have shown great power in maintaining norms against "the way of the world," even without legal support. On the other hand, insofar as we have present-day experience with the deregulation of time, it has taken place against norms that had legal support for a long period. That the world was not revolutionized immediately does not mean that more will not happen, once the effect of that legal support becomes merely a memory. Sunday is, in most states, no longer legally established as a day when no work is to be done, and yet most working Americans still do not work on Sunday. Is that a sign of countervailing institutional forces, or merely of a time lag?

Having acknowledged the methodological difficulty in finding data we can confidently rely on, we ought to be skeptical about the ability of social norms to produce a balanced use of time in America as it enters the twenty-first century. Even with legal support, the fabric of social time is fraying. The situation is exacerbated by a new sense of the competitiveness of the workplace, both among domestic workers and internationally. The tendency of this competition leads toward the aggrandizement of work time (both in terms of numbers of hours and in terms of its rhythm) at the cost of balance. There does not seem to be a comparable and countervailing resurgence of other institutional forces. Judging from the experience of workers exempt from the Fair Labor Standards Act, social norms do not seem strong enough to control these competitive pressures.

That there are problems with the freedom of time regime does not, of course, mean that the constructed time regime is problem-free. We cannot simply decide what the "right mix" of uses of time is and then make that the law; the criticisms recited earlier have a good deal of truth. No one wants to live in a lock-step society, and no one thinks that we could settle, once and for all, what a balanced society should look like. Moreover, the possibility for stipulating rules that fail to fit a large number of situations—that seriously chafe individuals or seriously misallocate social resources—is substantial. Finally, because this purposeful construction will depend on legislation, there is also the real danger that the law will reflect, not social wisdom, but merely the interests of the groups with the most political power.

What, then, could the proponent of constructed time say to soften the impact of these criticisms? Taking the last-named pitfall first, laws about time are undoubtedly the subject of political contest. We have seen the truth of that throughout this book, starting with the fact that even the drawing of the boundaries of the time zones continues to excite forces on one side or the other. This has both bad and good aspects. On the negative side, there is always the possibility that the resulting law will not represent a good solution to a particular aspect of the shaping of time, but only an attempt by one group to gain advantage. On the positive side, the reality of group jockeying may improve the outcome, by bringing to light ways in which an abstract proposal might not deal well with particular situations, and by mobilizing energy toward reshaping the law to a better fit. Sometimes it may be impossible to tell which is the case: does the continuing exemption of some agricultural workers from the Fair Labor Standards Act represent a "payoff" to powerful farming interests, or is it rather a recognition that the 40-hour week does not match the realities of some work that is highly seasonal and at times highly intensive? Overall, however, the present problem—how to achieve a balance among the time demands of the various institutions of the society—would seem to be a topic to which a political system based on group contestation, leavened by the power of the popular vote, is well suited. At the least, it seems that this process is more balanced than leaving matters to individual bargains in the market is likely to be. The most recent actual example of a political solution—the passage of the Family and Medical Leave Act in the early 1990s—was certainly highly contentious, but in the end it appears to represent compromise in its positive sense (an employee's right to some leave with job protection, but not with additional pay from the employer) rather than a mere division of spoils.[16] Certainly the FMLA has an intelligible, positive purpose; it is by no means a collection of disparate giveaways. And, once again, this is a situation in which the ideal statute would be contextual—would recognize the variety of social life and deal with it—rather than simply following an abstract principle to its logical conclusions.

Nevertheless, groups large enough to have an impact in the political arena are likely to submerge smaller differences that may be very important. "Labor" will have a voice, but surely all employees are not similarly situated. And the leadership in any group may be out of touch, or out of sympathy, with new ways of doing things. So there remains a real difficulty in building a constructed time regime that is at once sufficiently strong to create balance and yet sufficiently supple to allow for a diversity of ways of living and for the continued evolution of the society.

It is impossible to square this circle fully. Virtually by definition, any legislation regarding time that has bite will make some ways of organizing time easier than others. If it does not do so, it is useless. However, this inevitable bias can be tempered; it does not destroy the goal of flexible balance. The law, even when used to give structure to a situation, is more supple than is perhaps ordinarily understood.

As can be seen from the various mechanisms for giving structure to time that we have already examined, the law does not consist only of flat commands of required behavior. There are indeed some of these: "Close stores on Sunday!" or "Go to school 180 days in the year!" But these do not represent the most common time-shaping mechanisms. Many of the statutes that incorporate commands also provide for exceptions to those commands. Close stores on Sundays—but stores that cater to recreational activities can remain open. Go to school 180 days a year—but if you have an adequate plan for home education, you do not have to go to school in this lock-step fashion. Seen as a unit, a set of rules-plus-exceptions can allow considerably more flexibility than it might at first glance appear.

More important, there are many legal mechanisms for influencing behavior besides those that simply command. The law can provide a rule for governmental institutions which, by their pervasiveness, will influence what private actors will do—for instance, the stipulation that schools and courts and other public offices are closed on Saturdays and Sundays. The law can, without commanding or forbidding any particular behavior, create very powerful differential incentives for favored and disfavored ways of using time—it can, as the Fair Labor Standards Act does, and as various state statutes also do, create a structure for time and put different prices on work time in different parts of the structure. A somewhat similar approach would be to tax activities done at disfavored times, or to create tax incentives for favored possibilities.

Finally, even when the law does not itself decide, it can help choose who else will decide. This mechanism, as we have seen, operates powerfully at the boundary between work time and family time to favor the needs of employers rather than those of employees. While this is in part merely a reflection of private power enforced through neutral rules concerning agreements, it also represents a purposeful delegation of public authority, since the law gives priority to the decisions of some parties and not others. Since we can expect certain classes of decision-makers usually (although not uniformly) to decide issues in a certain way, a purposeful choice of delegatee can also help fashion the overall social structure we hope to achieve.

This variety of legal mechanisms gives us the power to shape time with considerable subtlety even within the framework of a constructed time regime. For example, let us suppose that the pressures to become a 24/7, around-the-clock economy materialize in the way that some have predicted, and let us further suppose that we are convinced that having very large numbers of people working at wildly disparate hours will have very bad consequences for family, civic, and social life. What should we do? The new information technology, and the globalization that has gone with it, do not necessarily have to produce business all day, every day; technology, by time-shifting activities, can also be used to support the differentiation of time. (E-commerce, for example, in contrast to both face-to-face sales and over-the-telephone orders, makes it possible for consumers to shop on Sunday and be served by employees who come to work on Monday.) We want laws that will set the goals of technology to reflect the broader social balance. At the same time, we cannot just forbid work between, say, the hours of 8:00 P.M. and 6:00 A.M. There is too much work that has to be done at that time, ranging from fire protection to the provision of basic utilities. And there is too much life that people want to live at night, ranging from going to the movies to eating in a restaurant, that requires some others to work then. Again, what should we do?

We have in fact many possibilities. We could have a general nighttime closing law but exempt from its operation specific trades. This has both the advantages and the disadvantages of particularity: only those situations which the legislature was convinced ought to be exempted, would be; but for just that reason the law might seem too confining. If so, we have many other tools we can use, which would create disincentives to nighttime work without specifying which particular needs are strong enough to surmount those disincentives. We could keep all schools and public buildings closed for their usual purposes at night, and help to set the tone of society in that indirect way. We could mandate that any work done at night be compensated by a time-and-a-half or double-time premium, which would create incentives for employers not to do at night anything that does not have to be done then. If we are afraid that this premium pay would create too strong a counter-incentive, leading employees to especially want to work at night, we could instead tax night work and give the bounty to the public. Or, instead of using financial measures, we could delegate the power to draw this particular boundary between work time and non-work time to workers rather than to employers, by providing that anyone who did not want to work at night was privileged not to, and could not be fired for exercising that privilege. Or, if we thought that maintaining family time (in the light of school time) was the most important objective, we could restrict the scope of the legal privilege to refuse nighttime work to those with children living at home. Which of these possibilities would be most effective in maintaining a zone of non-working time, and yet not be too restrictive, is of course a matter of fair debate. Each has its own wrinkles: some, for example, would influence the behavior of the self-employed, and some would not. But the idea that we must, or should, legally construct time only through blanket commands is surely wrong. Instead, it is some collection of mechanisms such as these, applied to various pressure points in our social structure of time, that constitutes the best version of a constructed time regime—best in the sense of providing a structure in which balance and diversity are both adequately (although not ideally) addressed.

Does this effort to work at the more nuanced edge of the constructed time regime collapse the distinction between it and the freedom of time regime? Insofar as we build a constructed time regime that reshapes time through the use of incentives rather than prohibitions, the distance between it and a freedom of time regime is somewhat lessened. The actual working of the system will depend on the actions of private parties: in what situations will they, for example, opt to pay premium rates or taxes? Still, we have done more than just construct the default rules of the freedom of time regime, because central features of the rules—just like the obligation to pay time-and-a-half under current law—cannot be evaded by bargaining. There remains a difference both in principle and in practice.

Neither the freedom of time regime nor the constructed time regime is perfect. Few social arrangements are. The merits and disadvantages of each regime depend in part on how the regime is implemented, which remains an imponderable. In the end, however, we face a fundamental choice. Is it worth having some restrictions placed on what we can do, in order to put in place a structure that helps us achieve individual and institutional balance in the use of time? Or is it better to do without the support of the law in giving explicit structure to our time, in order to be free to experiment with new and more individuated ways of shaping our lives?

Each reader can, of course, be the judge of which side is the stronger in the debate we have witnessed. I believe we are better off with some version of a constructed time regime, for three basic reasons. First, although the free choice promised by the freedom of time regime is very enticing, in the long run I think it will remain more promise than reality. Social norms in the absence of legal support will not prove sufficiently powerful to halt a slide toward an unbalanced dominance of work time. "Freedom of time" might well turn out to be a legalistic freedom experienced as freedom by only a few. Second, the real danger of the constructed time regime—too much regimentation, too much solidarity—seems to me not a realistic danger for our country in our present circumstances. The greater risk is that there will be too little support for many kinds of groups, especially for those not organized around the workplace, and too little support for individuals trying to achieve temporal balance. Finally, I am convinced that if we try to frame sensible laws, we can in fact provide enough support for balanced lives, while leaving enough room for individual action, that the extreme dangers in both directions can be avoided. In short, while we need continued experimentation as to what particular rules are best, we should not yield to the siren song of "choice" so as to seek to deregulate our system of time.

As the composer of Ecclesiastes described the balance of life— in words taken up and set to music many centuries later by Pete Seeger—there needs to be "a time for every purpose."[17] "A time" and not just "time"—structured time appropriate to the situation, and not just minutes. It is perhaps too much to hope that there will be a time for every purpose; but we ought to strive to create a time with its own form and dignity for each of the central purposes of life. A time to work—but also a time to nurture a family, to learn, to be an active participant in the culture, to participate in social and civic affairs. A central function of the law, especially in a society as wedded to the law as ours, is to help organize the society. As generations before us have tried to do, we, too, should use our power of creating law to help us shape a structure of time that will, in turn, help us to live fulfilled lives.

NOTES

1. THE LAW OF TIME

1. For the classic statement, see Emile Durkheim, *The Elementary Forms of Religious Life,* 8–10 (trans. Karen E. Fields; Free Press, 1995); compare the commentary on Durkheim's ideas about time offered in Steven Lukes, *Emile Durkheim,* 434–449 (Stanford University Press, 1985). For a more extensive review of the various positions that have been taken on the question of whether time is sui generis or socially constructed (or both), see Helga Nowotny, "Time and Social Theory," 1 *Time and Society* 421 (1992).

2. Genesis 1:5 (Revised Standard Version).

3. Pitirim A. Sorokin, *Sociocultural Causality, Space, Time,* 192–193 (Duke University Press, 1943).

4. Regarding the general approach of describing time in terms of the operations performed with it, see Pitirim A. Sorokin and Robert K. Merton, "Social Time: A Methodological and Functional Analysis," 42 *American Journal of Sociology* 615 (1937).

5. Daniel J. Boorstin, *The Discoverers,* 39 (Random House, 1983)

6. Nishimoto Ikuku, "The 'Civilization' of Time: Japan and the Adoption of the Western Time System," 6 *Time and Society* 237 (1997).

7. Several other authors have found it useful to talk of time in terms of its having several dimensions, although the lists, drawn for different

purposes, are not congruent with the one given here. See, e.g., Robert Levine, *A Geography of Time*, 3 (Basic Books, 1997) (rhythms, sequences, synchronies, and tempos); Eviatar Zerubavel, *Hidden Rhythms*, 1 (University of California Press, 1985) (sequential structure, duration, temporal location, and rate of recurrence); and Jeremy Rifkin, *Time Wars*, 48 (Henry Holt and Co., 1987) (sequential structure, duration, planning, rate of recurrence, synchronization, and temporal perspective).

It is sometimes said that whole cultures are dominated by one conception of time or another, and in this regard modern cultures are said to have a linear conception of time, in which long-term change and progress are possible, as contrasted with traditional cultures, which are said to have a cyclical conception of time in which the essential features of life recur over long periods. See the discussions in Carol J. Greenhouse, *A Moment's Notice*, 30ff. (Cornell University Press, 1996), and David M. Engel, "Law, Time, and Community," 21 *Law & Society Review* 605, 609–610 (1987). This distinction seems overly simplistic; see Zerubavel, *Hidden Rhythms*, 112ff. At least with regard to the workaday time tasks with which the law deals, elements of linear and cyclical thinking are both endemic even in modern societies.

For a more general discussion of various views of time and how they might influence the law, see Rebecca R. French, "Time in the Law," 72 *University of Colorado Law Review* 663 (2001).

8. Other ways of organizing time are often treated, even praised, as mere anachronism; e.g., Nicholas J. Mount, "Baseball Time," 3 *Time and Society* 377 (1994).

9. For sources on the misdescription of complexity as "scarcity" of time, see Werner Bergmann, "The Problem of Time in Sociology," 1 *Time and Society* 81, 108 (1992).

2. TELLING TIME

1. Department of Transportation, "Relocation of Standard Time Zone Boundary in the State of Kentucky," 65 Fed. Reg. 50154 (Aug. 17, 2000); the quotation is at 65 Fed. Reg. 50157. For another, similar proceeding, see Department of Transportation, "Standard Time Zone Boundary in the State of Indiana," 56 Fed. Reg. 51997 (Oct. 17, 1991).

2. For a diagrammatic presentation of the variations, see Derek Howse, *Greenwich Time and the Discovery of the Longitude,* 38 (Oxford University Press, 1980).

3. Ian R. Bartky, *Selling The True Time,* 60–61 (Stanford University Press, 2000).

4. Michael O'Malley, *Keeping Watch,* 76 (Smithsonian Institution Press, 1990); Bartky, *Selling the True Time,* 97.

5. Howse, *Greenwich Time,* 120.

6. O'Malley, *Keeping Watch,* 96.

7. Clark Blaise, *Time Lord,* 85 (Pantheon Books, 2000); Duncan Steel, *Marking Time,* 262–264 (John Wiley & Sons, 2000).

8. Howse, *Greenwich Time,* 67.

9. S. Rep. No. 840, 47th Cong., 1st Sess. 2 (1882).

10. O'Malley, *Keeping Watch,* 100.

11. Ibid., 111.

12. Bartky, *Selling the True Time,* 1–2.

13. On the international tussles, stretching into the twentieth century, on whether Greenwich or some other place should furnish the starting point, see Howse, *Greenwich Time,* 127–156.

14. Information in this paragraph is drawn from O'Malley, *Keeping Watch,* 111–123.

15. Responses are discussed in ibid., 123–144.

16. For examples of the other lines of cases, compare the opinion of Justice Holmes of Massachusetts in the case of Clapp v. Jenkins, reported in the *New York Times,* December 5, 1883, 4 (favoring time-zone time, which had just come into effect) with Searles v. Averhoff, 28 Neb. 668, 44 N.W. 872 (1890) (favoring "common time"), both dealing with court procedural rules; for selling liquor after hours, see State v. Johnson, 74 Minn. 381, 77 N.W. 293 (1898); Salt Lake City v. Robinson, 39 Utah 260, 116 P. 442 (1911) (both favoring time-zone time).

17. 110 Iowa 75, 81 N.W. 188 (1899).

18. Jones, 81 N.W. at 189.

19. Ibid.

20. Ibid.

21. Ibid.

22. Ibid.

23. Ibid.

24. 120 Ky. 752, 87 S.W. 1115 (1905).

25. Rochester German Ins. Co., 87 S.W. at 1118–19.

26. Ibid., 1117.

27. Ibid.

28. Ibid., 1117–18.

29. Ch. 24, 40 Stat. 450 (1918).

30. 15 U.S.C. §261 (2000). The current legal definitions of American time zones can be found at 49 C.F.R. Subtitle A, §71.1 et seq. (2001).

31. Whether time-zone time is, even at this date, optional for the states depends on the construction of the later-added daylight-saving provisions, 15 U.S.C. §260a (2000); needless to say, no case has arisen to press the point.

32. Eviatar Zerubavel, "The Standardization of Time: A Sociohistorical Perspective," 88 *American Journal of Sociology* no. 1, 1–23 (July 1982).

33. Regarding the two types of solidarity referred to in this paragraph, see Emile Durkheim, *The Division of Labor in Society* (trans. George Simpson; The Free Press, 1964) ("mechanical" and "organic" solidarity).

34. Zerubavel, "Standardization," 15.

35. Ian R. Bartky and Elizabeth Harrison, "Standard and Daylight-saving Time," 240 *Scientific American* no. 5, 46, 49 (May 1979).

36. Ibid., 49 and map at 51.

37. Standard Time Zone Investigation, 34th Supp. Rep., 309 I.C.C. 780, 796 (1960).

38. E.g., ibid., 785–786.

39. Standard Time Zone Investigation, 21st Supp. Rep., 218 I.C.C. 221, 228 (1936).

40. O'Malley, *Keeping Watch*, 267.

41. Thomas E. Pyne, *Standard Time*, 1 (Interstate Commerce Commission, 1958). There had been some local experiments earlier, especially in cities on the eastern edges of time zones, where standard time was nearly one-half hour behind solar time and therefore had a "daylight losing" effect. O'Malley, *Keeping Watch*, 263–267.

42. Ch. 51, 41 Stat. 280 (1919).

43. Massachusetts State Grange v. Benton, 272 U.S. 525 (1926), affirming 10 F.2d 515 (1st Cir. 1925).

44. Ch. 8, 56 Stat. 9 (1942). The Act provided that daylight saving would end six months after the termination of the war, but Congress in fact ended it sooner, in 1945. Ch. 388, 59 Stat. 537 (1945). The World War II Act, in contrast to that for the First World War, made daylight-saving time a year-round proposition.

45. A map displaying the various combinations appears in Bartky and Harrison, "Standard and Daylight-saving Time," 51.

46. P.L. 89-387, 80 Stat. 107 (1966), codified at 15 U.S.C. §260 et seq. (2000).

47. The 1966 Act provided for daylight saving to extend from the last Sunday in April to the last Sunday of October. In 1986, daylight saving was enlarged to begin on the first Sunday in April. P.L. 99-359, 100 Stat. 764 (1986), codified at 15 U.S.C. §260a(a) (2000).

48. P.L. 92-267, 86 Stat. 116 (1972), codified at 15 U.S.C. §260a(a) (2000).

49. 1B Ariz. Rev. Stat. Ann. §1-242 (1995); Haw. Rev. Stat. Ann. §1-31 (2000).

50. Ind. Code §1-1-8.1-1&2 (1998).

51. This rationale, however, continues to be asserted. Three of the four congressional findings made in 1986 to support the extension of daylight saving by a month asserted its real or potential virtues as an energy conservation measure. P.L. 99-359, 100 Stat. 764, §2 (1986).

52. O'Malley, *Keeping Watch*, 256–308.

53. The parallels are nicely developed in ibid., 295–308.

54. Example from ibid., 283.

55. Ibid., 292.

56. Ibid., 291.

57. Ibid., 293; see Allied Theatre Owners of Indiana, Inc. v. Volpe, 426 F.2d 1002 (7th Cir. 1970).

58. On the resistance of those on the western sides of time zones even to wartime daylight saving, see Pyne, *Standard Time*, 4.

59. O'Malley, *Keeping Watch*, 289–290.

60. Statement of the Advisory Commission on Intergovernmental Relations forwarded to the House Committee on Interstate and Foreign

Commerce on February 3, 1966, 2 U.S. Code, Cong. and Admin. News, 89th Cong., 2d Sess. 2120, 2122 (1966).

61. H.R. Report No. 1315 (March 10, 1966), 2 U.S. Code, Cong. and Admin. News, 89th Cong., 2d Sess. 2111 (1966).

62. Ibid., 2113.

63. For further background on the need for the uniformity ultimately provided by the 1966 Act, see Department of Transportation, *Standard Time in the United States,* 7–11 (1970).

64. Blaise, *Time Lord,* 180 (quoting Sandford Fleming).

65. On the very small differences between UTC and GMT, see Howse, *Greenwich Time,* 172–190.

66. Bruce D. Callander, "Zulu Time," *Air Force Magazine,* October 1991, 78, 80.

67. For basic information, see the NIST Web site on time, *www.boulder. nist.gov/timefreq* (last consulted on 9/30/01).

68. Blaise, *Time Lord,* 185.

69. Michael Yaki, "Midnight on Equal Time," *New York Times,* December 8, 1999, A31.

70. Karl H. Horning, Daniela Ahrens, and Anette Gerhard, "Do Technologies Have Time?" 8 *Time and Society* 293 (1999).

3. COMMUNITY AND FAMILY TIME

1. An Act for the Service of Almighty God and the Establishment of the Protestant Religion within this Province, 13 *Archives of Maryland* 425, reprinted in McGowan v. Maryland, 366 U.S. 420, 446 & n.19 (1961).

2. Md. Code Ann., Art. 27, §492 (1957).

3. Ibid., §521.

4. McGowan v. Maryland, 366 U.S. 420 (1961).

5. Md. Code Ann., Business Regulation §18-101 (1999).

6. Gustavus Myers, "Blue Laws," *Encyclopedia of the Social Sciences,* II, 600–601 (Macmillan, 1930).

7. David N. Laband and Deborah H. Heinbuch, *Blue Laws,* 8 (D. C. Heath, 1987).

8. Appendix II to the Opinion of Mr. Justice Frankfurter in McGowan, 366 U.S. at 551 et seq.

9. McGowan, 366 U.S. at 435.

10. Ibid., 366 U.S. at 496.

11. Exodus 20:8 (Revised Standard Version).

12. Ibid., verse 11.

13. "The meaning of the Sabbath," it has been justly said, "is to celebrate time rather than space." Abraham J. Heschel, "The Sabbath," 10, in Heschel, *The Earth Is the Lord's and The Sabbath* (World Publishing Company, 1963).

14. Eviatar Zerubavel, *The Seven Day Circle*, 44–59 (University of Chicago Press, 1989); Pitirim A. Sorokin and Robert K. Merton, "Social Time: A Methodological and Functional Analysis," 42 *American Journal of Sociology* 615, 624–645 (1937).

15. Zerubavel, *Seven Day Circle*, 23.

16. Ibid., 20.

17. Ibid., 22–23.

18. Ibid., 28–29.

19. Ibid., 33–34.

20. Exodus 23:12 (Revised Standard Version).

21. A point well made in Christopher Hill, "The Uses of Sabbatarianism," chap. 5 of *Society and Puritanism in Pre-Revolutionary England* (Secker & Warburg, 1964), 124–125.

22. 366 U.S. 420 (1961).

23. Ibid. at 431.

24. U.S. Constitution, Amendment I, made applicable to the states by U.S. Constitution, Amendment XIV.

25. McGowan, 366 U.S. at 448.

26. Ibid. at 450.

27. Ibid. at 477.

28. Ibid. at 506.

29. Ibid. at 507.

30. Braunfeld v. Brown, 366 U.S. 599 (1961).

31. Gallagher v. Crown Kosher Super Market, 366 U.S. 617 (1961).

32. 366 U.S. 599 (1961).

33. Braunfeld, 366 U.S. at 607.

34. Ibid. at 608. The Court also argued that recognizing this exemption might cause Sunday observers to complain that they were being

disadvantaged; and if the answer to that were that the exemption would be open only to those who were conscientiously following their faith, then the government might get entangled in determining who was a true believer. Ibid. at 608–609.

35. Douglas, J., dissenting in McGowan, 366 U.S. at 572–573.

36. Brennan, J., concurring and dissenting in Braunfeld, 366 U.S. at 614.

37. Alexis McCrossen, *Holy Day, Holiday: The American Sunday,* 62 (Cornell University Press, 2000).

38. Ibid., 71.

39. Ibid., 71–78.

40. Ibid., 96–102.

41. Ibid., 91–92; 127. For another, concurring treatment of the matters covered in this paragraph, see Alan Raucher, "Sunday Business and the Decline of Sunday Closing Laws: A Historical Overview," 36 *Journal of Church and State* 13, 21–22 (1994).

42. See Jerome A. Barron, "Sunday in North America," 79 *Harvard Law Review* 42, 49–50 (1965).

43. 472 U.S. 703 (1985).

44. Ibid. at 706.

45. Nevertheless, statutes allowing employees to choose their day of rest and requiring employers to respect that choice remain on the books—e.g., Maryland Code Ann., Labor and Employment §3-704 (1999).

46. McGowan, 366 U.S. at 506.

47. This and succeeding paragraphs on the Soviet experiment derive from Zerubavel, *Seven Day Circle,* 35–43; William Chase and Lewis Siegelbaum, "Worktime and Industrialization in the U.S.S.R., 1917–1941," in Gary Cross, ed., *Worktime and Industrialization,* 183, 197–206 (Temple University Press, 1988); and "The Continuous Working Week in Soviet Russia," 23 *International Labour Review* 157 (1931).

48. Chase and Siegelbaum, "Worktime and Industrialization in the U.S.S.R.," 203 (quoting V. V. Kuibyshev).

49. Zerubavel, *Seven Day Circle,* 38.

50. Quoted by Justice Frankfurter in McGowan, 366 U.S. at 482 (speaker not identified by name).

51. Timothy Aeppel, "More Plants Go 24/7, and Workers Are Left at Sixes and Sevens," *Wall Street Journal*, July 24, 2001, A1.

52. See Robert D. Putnam, "Bowling Alone: America's Declining Social Capital," 6 *Journal of Democracy* no. 1, 65 (1995).

53. Emile Durkheim, *The Elementary Forms of Religious Life*, 8–10 (trans. Karen Fields; The Free Press, 1995); Pitirim A. Sorokin, *Sociocultural Causality, Space, Time*, 172–173 (Duke University Press, 1943); Eviatar Zerubavel, *Hidden Rhythms*, 64–67 (University of California Press, 1985); Zerubavel, *Seven Day Circle*, 22–23.

54. See Putnam, "Bowling Alone," 65, 67–73.

55. E.g., Caldor's, Inc. v. Bedding Barn, Inc., 177 Conn. 304, 417 A.2d 343 (1979) (in addition to making statutory distinctions that seemed unrelated to maintaining a day of rest but very related to maintaining various commercial advantages, the Act as a whole exempted, in one way or another, about 938,000 workers out of a total state work force of 1,450,940). For further citations, see Neil J. Dilloff, "Never on Sunday: The Blue Laws Controversy," 39 *Maryland Law Review* 679, 681 n.11 (1980).

56. Dilloff, "Never on Sunday," 680.

57. Jamie Price and Bruce Yandle, "Labor Markets and Sunday Closing Laws," 8 *Journal of Labor Research* 407 (1987).

58. Laband and Heinbuch, *Blue Laws*, 50. These authors also repeat, on p. 162, the apparently contradictory figures of Price and Yandle, "Labor Markets and Sunday Closing Laws."

59. 36 U.S.C. §104 (Supp. V 1999).

60. 36 U.S.C. §129 (Supp. V 1999).

61. 36 U.S.C. §127 (Supp. V 1999).

62. 5 U.S.C. §6103 (2000).

63. For details on the effect of legal holidays on procedural rules, see Charles A. Wright and Arthur R. Miller, *Federal Practice and Procedure* 4A, §§1162 and 1163 (1987).

64. P.L. 98-144, 97 Stat. 917 (1983).

65. N.H. RSA §288:1 and notes thereto (1999 and Supp. 2001).

66. Bureau of National Affairs, *Basic Patterns in Union Contracts*, 59 (14th ed., 1995).

67. The law of holidays is often treated as a subsidiary of the law of Sundays, for example by some of the treatises. See, e.g., *American Jurisprudence 2d*, whose relevant category is "Sunday and Holidays," 73 *American Jurisprudence 2d* 775 (1974 and Supp. 2001).

68. 1962 Mass. Acts ch. 616, §5.

69. Ibid., §13.

70. See Mass. Ann. Laws ch. 136, §6, cl. 50; §13 (1989).

71. 1994 Mass. Acts ch. 193, codified at Mass. G.L. ch. 136, §16 (2000).

72. The list of legal holidays to which the various exclusions should be compared is set out in Mass. G.L. ch. 4, §7, cl. 18 (2000).

73. Raucher, "Sunday Business and the Decline of Sunday Closing Laws," 13.

74. See Price and Yandle, "Labor Markets and Sunday Closing Laws," 412–413.

75. Raucher, "Sunday Business and the Decline of Sunday Closing Laws," 31.

76. For the debate on this point, see Gordon Tullock, "The Transitional Gains Trap," 6 *Bell Journal of Economics* 671 (1975); John C. Moorhouse, "Is Tullock Correct about Sunday Closing Laws?" 42 *Public Choice* 197 (1984); J. A. Kay and C. N. Morris, "The Economic Efficiency of Sunday Trading Restrictions," 36 *The Journal of Industrial Economics* 113 (1987); and Douglas W. McNiel and Shirley S. Yu, "Blue Laws: Impact on Regional Retail Activity," 8 *Population Research and Policy Review* 267 (1989).

Following the repeal of Blue Laws in Texas in 1985, the state comptroller's office apparently embarked on a serious effort to analyze sales data to determine the effect of repeal on retail sales, but the report was never released because the effect of the legal change was confounded by a simultaneous general economic downturn. See Donna Steph Hansard, "'Old Blue' Is Gone, But New Blues Are Here: Economic Downturn Spoils Test of Numbers," *Dallas Morning News*, September 14, 1986, 2H.

77. Kenneth A. Sommer, "Sunday Closing Laws in the United States: An Unconstitutional Anachronism," 11 *Suffolk University Law Review* 1089, 1092–93 (1977).

78. Donna Steph Hansard, "Anti-Blue Law Group Gains Members," *Dallas Morning News*, March 22, 1985, 3E.

79. Chris Reidy and Peter J. Howe, "Firms Fight Ballot Issues with Bucks," *Boston Globe*, September 10, 1994, 1.

80. Maine: Maine Bureau of Corporations, Elections, and Commissions, General Election Tabulation for the Election of November 6, 1990, Official Vote for Initiative Question (272,129 votes for repeal, 246,378 against); Massachusetts: Office of the Massachusetts Secretary of the Commonwealth, Massachusetts Election Statistics 1994, 499 (1,100,994 votes for repeal, 990,057 against).

81. This paragraph is drawn from McCrossen, *Holy Day, Holiday,* 12–15 and 136–151; quotation on p. 150.

4. Work Time

1. Upton v. JWP Businessland, 425 Mass. 756, 682 N.E.2d 1357 (1997).

2. Brief for Plaintiff/Appellant at 20–21, Upton v. JWP Businessland, 425 Mass. 756, 682 N.E.2d 1357 (1997).

3. Upton, 682 N.E.2d at 1359.

4. Upton, 682 N.E.2d at 1360.

5. See Lloyd v. AMF Bowling Centers, Inc., 195 Ariz. 144, 985 P.2d 629 (App. Div. 1999); Daley v. Aetna Life and Casualty Co., 249 Conn. 766, 734 A.2d 112 (1999); Pasqua v. Thomson Interactive Media, 2000 WL 1763707 (Conn. Super., October 31, 2000) (unreported decision).

6. 29 U.S.C. §201 et seq. (2000).

7. 29 U.S.C. §207 (a)(1) (2000).

8. E. P. Thompson, "Time, Work-Discipline, and Industrial Capitalism," 38 *Past and Present* 56, 56–60 (1967).

9. Ibid., 73.

10. David R. Roediger and Philip S. Foner, *Our Own Time,* 123 (Greenwood Press, 1989).

11. 198 U.S. 45 (1905).

12. Ibid., 61.

13. 208 U.S. 412 (1908).

14. Roediger and Foner, *Our Own Time,* 177.

15. Ibid., 177–207.

16. Quoted in ibid., 191.

17. David R. Roediger, "The Limits of Corporate Reform: Fordism, Taylorism, and the Working Week in the United States, 1914–1929," in Gary Cross, ed., *Worktime and Industrialization,* 142–148 (Temple University Press, 1988).

18. Roediger and Foner, *Our Own Time,* 237–241.

19. Ibid., 243.

20. S.5267, 72d Cong., 2d Sess., 76 Cong. Rec. 820 (1932).

21. Roediger and Foner, *Our Own Time,* 247–250.

22. Ch. 90, 48 Stat. 195 (1933).

23. Joseph S. Zeisel, "The Workweek in American Industry 1850–1956," 81 *Monthly Labor Review* no. 1, 23, 25 (1958).

24. Roediger and Foner, *Our Own Time,* 249–250; Benjamin K. Hunnicutt, *Work Without End,* 175–178 (Temple University Press, 1988).

25. Hunnicutt, *Work Without End,* 178–190.

26. Ch. 881, 49 Stat. 2036 (1936).

27. Hunnicutt, *Work Without End,* 242–249.

28. Ch. 676, 52 Stat. 1060, §7(a) (1938).

29. Zeisel, "The Workweek in American Industry," 25.

30. Ch. 676, 52 Stat. 1060, §13(a)(6) (1938).

31. Ibid., §13(a) and (b).

32. Ibid., §2(a).

33. For example, while the Act foresees that its application to apprentices and those learning a trade must be limited—for few employers will hire them at full minimum wage—it interposes the judgment of the Administrator of the Wage and Hour Division of the Department of Labor, who is empowered to set the terms of such arrangements. Ibid., §14. Presumably his job is to prevent oppression in a situation where the weaker party will not be able to protect itself. The same approach is taken in large part to defining what employment of teenagers constitutes "oppressive child labor." Ibid., §3(l).

The principal counter-example is the enormous exclusion of "any employee employed in agriculture." Ibid., §13(a)(6). Was this exclusion based on the idea that agricultural hours are very variable, and cannot be as easily fit within a regimented time pattern as can industrial work? Or that agricultural hours always have been and always will be more than 40 per week? It hardly seems, given the conditions of the 1930s, that it could have been based on the theory that agricultural laborers had the bargaining power to take care of themselves. Perhaps it represents the extreme opposite case: workers who were so powerless and unorganized (and, for many, so subordinated by the regime of Jim Crow) that they could protect themselves neither in the marketplace nor in the halls of Congress. If so, it is consistent with the yet broader notion that Congress did not intend, when it passed the Fair Labor Standards Act, to revamp society.

34. Robert L. Stern and R. S. Smethurst, "How the Supreme Court May View the Fair Labor Standards Act," 6 *Law and Contemporary Problems* 431 (1939).

35. United States v. Darby, 312 U.S. 100 (1941), overruling Hammer v. Dagenhart, 247 U.S. 251 (1918).

36. S.5267, 72d Cong., 2d Sess., 76 Cong. Rec. 820 (1932).

37. Carroll R. Daugherty, "The Economic Coverage of the Fair Labor Standards Act: A Statistical Study," 6 *Law and Contemporary Problems* 406, 407 (1939).

38. There were 54+ million people in the civilian labor force in 1938; of these, 44+ million were employed. U.S. Bureau of the Census, *Historical Statistics of the United States, Colonial Times to 1957*, 70 (1960) (Series D 1-12).

39. Daugherty, "The Economic Coverage of the Fair Labor Standards Act," 407.

40. For a graphic demonstration of the effect of World War II and the changed circumstances following the war, see Zeisel, "The Workweek in American Industry," 26.

41. Roediger and Foner, *Our Own Time*, 234–236.

42. See the chart in Willis J. Nordlund, "A Brief History of the Fair Labor Standards Act," 39 *Labor Law Journal* 715, 725 (1988).

43. Ch. 676, 52 Stat. 1060, §13(a)(1) and (2) (1938).

44. For details, see Susan Schechter, *Fair Labor Standards Act Explained*, 49–50 and 92ff. (CCH, 1997).

45. Government workers were not listed in the Act's "Exemptions," but the same result was reached by defining "employer," the initial coverage term, not to include governments. Ch. 676, 52 Stat. 1060, §3(d) (1938).

46. For details, see Schechter, *Fair Labor Standards Act Explained*, 54ff. The Supreme Court's consideration of whether and how the FLSA is enforceable against state and local governments can only be labeled "zigzag." The latest word, Alden v. Maine, 527 U.S. 706 (1999), leaves the Act enforceable although, as against the States, only with difficulty.

47. U.S. Department of Labor, *Minimum Wage and Maximum Hours Standards Under the Fair Labor Standards Act*, Table 10, p. 33 (1993). The overall data for 1990 were revised somewhat in a later report, but no similar breakdown was offered. See U.S. Department of Labor, *Minimum Wage and Overtime Hours Under the Fair Labor Standards Act*, Table C1d90, p. 126 (1998).

48. Roediger and Foner, *Our Own Time*, 274.

49. Juliet B. Schor, *The Overworked American* (Basic Books, 1992). My references are to the paperback edition (1993).

50. Ibid., 29.

51. Ibid..

52. Ibid., 30.

53. Ibid., 35.

54. Ibid., 59–68.

55. John P. Robinson and Geoffrey Godbey, *Time for Life* (Pennsylvania State University Press, 1997).

56. Ibid., 95.

57. Ibid., 105.

58. Ibid., 108.

59. Ibid., 127.

60. Ibid., 145.

61. For what it is worth, both books seem to differ from the federal government's own view of the matter, at least as reported in its most widely circulated form, the *Statistical Abstract*. Although this source does not provide a composite figure, we find there that, on an annual average basis, wage and salary workers (both agricultural and non-agricultural) worked about an hour a week more in 1990 than in 1970, while self-employed workers (both agricultural and non-agricultural)

worked about 4 hours a week less. (These figures are for paid work only.) U.S. Department of Commerce, *Statistical Abstract of the United States: 2000*, 410, Table 656.

62. Schor, *The Overworked American*, 30.

63. Ibid.

64. Robinson and Godbey, *Time for Life*, 127 and 128. I should mention that, as a matter of policy, Robinson and Godbey agree with Schor on the importance of vacation time. Activities as diverse as reading and playing sports occupy a much larger portion of free time on vacation days than they do during the normal week; TV much less (pp. 310–311). Europeans, equally prosperous and modern as Americans, have much more vacation and holiday time. "On this point we agree with Juliet Schor about Americans being overworked" (p. 298).

65. Robinson and Godbey, *Time for Life*, 335 (2d ed., 1999).

66. U.S. Bureau of the Census, *Statistical Abstract of the United States: 2000*, 410, Table 656.

67. Philip L. Rones, Randy E. Ilg, and Jennifer M. Gardner, "Trends in Hours of Work Since the Mid-1970's," 120 *Monthly Labor Review* no. 4, 3, 7 (April 1997).

68. Ibid., 8.

69. Ibid.

70. See David Kennedy, *Freedom from Fear*, 652 (Oxford University Press, 1999).

71. For evidence on this point, see Schor, *The Overworked American*, 66–68.

72. Rones, Ilg, and Gardner, "Trends in Hours of Work," 9.

73. There are four groups of workers in which more than 30 percent have very-long-hour jobs: managers, professionals, sales workers, and transportation workers. Ibid., 9. The first two groups are fully exempt, as discussed in the text. Transportation workers and sales workers also lack the full protection of the Act: the former because many fall under special exemptions, and the latter because those who work mostly on commissions do not receive time-and-a-half.

74. 29 U.S.C. §213(a)(1) (2000).

75. U.S. Department of Labor, *Minimum Wage and Overtime Hours Under the Fair Labor Standards Act*, 21–22 and 26 (1998).

76. Rones, Ilg, and Gardner, "Trends in Hours of Work," 9.

77. What history there is, is set out in Deborah C. Malamud, "Engineering the Middle Classes: Class Line-Drawing in New Deal Hours Legislation," 96 *Michigan Law Review* 2212 (1998); the direct legislative history of the FLSA is discussed on pp. 2286–2289.

78. P.L. 104-188 §2105(a), 110 Stat. 1929 (1996), codified at 29 U.S.C. §213(a)(17) (2000).

79. See generally Po Bronson, *The Nudist on the Late Shift* (Random House, 1999).

80. Juliet B. Schor, "Worktime in Contemporary Context: Amending the Fair Labor Standards Act," 70 *Chicago-Kent Law Review* 157, 170 (1994).

81. Ellen Galinsky, Stacy S. Kim, and James T. Bond, *Feeling Overworked: When Work Becomes Too Much*, 7 (Families and Work Institute, 2001).

82. See Douglas McCollam, "Father Time," *The American Lawyer*, December 1999, 115 (story of Reginald Heber Smith, creator of the lawyers' time-keeping system).

83. 5 U.S.C. §5542 et seq. (2000). Whether the Department of Justice was subject to this rule, and if so how to implement it, has been the subject of recent litigation, John Doe v. United States, No. 98-896C in the Court of Claims. The complaint against the government was supported by a copy of a high-level, internal DOJ memo written in 1980 which concluded that the DOJ was obligated to pay overtime. Memorandum of Leon Ulman, Deputy Assistant Attorney General, dated April 21, 1980. Some other federal agencies have already been operating under this interpretation of the statute without judicial compulsion.

84. Kennedy, *Freedom from Fear*, 777.

85. Arlie R. Hochschild, *The Time Bind*, 6 (Henry Holt, 1997).

86. Rones, Ilg, and Gardner, "Trends in Hours of Work," 11.

87. Arlie R. Hochschild, *The Time Bind* (Henry Holt, 1997).

88. Ibid., 25–30. Hochschild also presents some evidence to support the claim that these findings are true of workers in American companies in general.

89. Ibid., 28–34. Some reviewers of the book questioned whether Hochschild's own data did not undermine the supposed family-

friendliness of the company. See, e.g., Jerry Jacobs, "Review," 104 *American Journal of Sociology* 1563, 1564 (1999).

90. Hochschild, *The Time Bind*, 217.

91. Schor, "Worktime in Contemporary Context," 165, 167.

92. Harriet B. Presser, "Toward a 24-Hour Economy," 284 *Science* 1778, 1779 (1999).

93. Schor was optimistic that the shorter hours she recommended would be more efficient hours, so that income would not suffer; but her data were (perhaps necessarily) thin. See Schor, "Worktime in Contemporary Context," 167–168; Schor, *The Overworked American*, 152–157.

94. Useful data were collected in 1985, 1991, and 1997 as special additions to the continuous Current Population Survey. For various reasons—including the asking of somewhat different questions—the results are not completely comparable. Some useful reports, in chronological order, are the following: Shirley J. Smith, "The Growing Diversity of Work Schedules," 109 *Monthly Labor Review* no. 11, 7 (November 1986); Daniel S. Hamermesh, *Workdays, Workhours and Work Schedules* (W. E. Upjohn Institute for Employment Research, 1996); U.S. Department of Labor, Bureau of Labor Statistics, "Workers on Flexible and Shift Schedules," News Release USDL 98-119 (3/26/98; *http://stats.bls.gov/newsrels. htm*); Presser, "Toward a 24-Hour Economy"; Thomas M. Beers, "Flexible Schedules and Shift Work: Replacing the '9-to-5' Workday?" 123 *Monthly Labor Review* no. 6, 33 (June 2000).

95. U.S. Department of Labor, "Workers on Flexible and Shift Schedules," Table 5.

96. Beers, "Flexible Schedules and Shift Work," 37; Presser, "Toward a 24-Hour Economy," 1779 (giving slightly different figures).

97. Beers, "Flexible Schedules and Shift Work," 38.

98. The data are usefully graphed by Hamermesh, *Workdays, Workhours and Work Schedules*, 45.

99. Ibid., 46–70.

100. Ibid., 66.

101. Smith, "The Growing Diversity of Work Schedules," 8; Hamermesh, *Workdays, Workhours and Work Schedules*, 21. The lower figures reported in Presser, "Toward a 24-Hour Economy," 1779, are on this point

not comparable since they report not only working five days a week but also only working weekdays.

102. Smith, "The Growing Diversity of Work Schedules," 12; Hamermesh, *Workdays, Workhours and Work Schedules,* 47.

103. Presser, "Toward a 24-Hour Economy," 1779. It is not clear whether the lower figures for weekend work reported in Hamermesh, *Workdays, Workhours and Work Schedules,* 47, are based on methodological or historical differences.

104. See Smith, "The Growing Diversity of Work Schedules," 12; Hamermesh, *Workdays, Workhours and Work Schedules,* 47.

105. The Walsh-Healey Act (41 U.S.C. §35) (1994) and the Contract Workers Hours and Safety Standards Act (40 U.S.C. §328) (1994)—each of which covers work on U.S. government contracts—were amended to eliminate their 8-hour-day provisions when the federal government flextime program was put into place. P.L. 99-145, §1241, 99 Stat. 734 (1985) ("Flextime For Federal Contractor Employees").

106. The FLSA does not preempt more restrictive state statutes. 29 U.S.C. §218(a) (2000). As of 1995, six states (Alabama, Alaska, California, Colorado, Nevada, and Wyoming) required overtime pay after a certain number of hours per day had been reached. Daniel V. Yager and Sandra J. Boyd, "Reinventing the Fair Labor Standards Act to Support the Reengineered Workplace," 11 *The Labor Lawyer* 321, 323 and n.7 (1995). Three—Alabama, Colorado, and Wyoming—repealed their requirements shortly thereafter.

107. Beers, "Flexible Schedules and Shift Work," 34.

108. Ibid., 40.

109. Presser, "Toward a 24-Hour Economy," 1778.

110. See Hamermesh, *Workdays, Workhours and Work Schedules,* 1–9.

111. Beers, "Flexible Schedules and Shift Work," 40.

112. The Bureau of National Affairs, *Basic Patterns in Union Contracts,* 52 (14th ed., 1995).

113. Some states already have statutes providing for premium weekend pay for government workers, or for those working on government contracts; e.g., Haw. Rev. Stat. Ann. §104-2(c) (2000) (Hawaii); Or. Rev. Stat. §279.334 (Supp. 1998) (Oregon).

114. There is also something to be said from the point of view of distributive justice for giving premium pay for night work at least. People who work at night are generally worse off than those who do not. See Hamermesh, *Workdays, Workhours and Work Schedules*, 51–57.

5. SCHOOL TIME

1. P.L. 102-62, §102, 105 Stat. 305 (1991).

2. National Education Commission on Time and Learning, *Prisoners of Time*, 7 (1994).

3. Ibid., 8.

4. U.S. Bureau of the Census, *Profile of General Demographic Characteristics for the United States: 2000* (available on the Census Bureau Web site, *www.census.gov*, 7/10/01).

5. U.S. Bureau of the Census, *Enrollment Status of the Population 3 Years Old and Over, by Age, Sex, Race, Hispanic Origin, Nativity, and Selected Educational Characteristics: October 2000* (available on the Census Bureau Web site, *www.census.gov*, 7/10/01). An additional 23.5 million people were enrolled in nursery school, kindergarten, or college. Ibid.

6. James A. Rapp, *Education Law*, Vol. 3, §8.03[1], [5] (Matthew Bender, 2001). The state statutes are listed and briefly described in ibid., vol. 7, Table T4.

7. Ibid., Vol. 3, §.8.03[8].

8. Pierce v. Society of Sisters, 268 U.S. 510 (1925).

9. Computed from data for 1998 in U.S. Bureau of the Census, *Statistical Abstract of the United States: 2000*, 156, Table 247.

10. State-by-state details of the minimum required number of days and length of days in the school calendar, and of policies regarding the start day for the school year, can be found in Council of Chief State School Officers, *Key State Education Policies on K–12 Education: 2000*, a report of a biennial survey posted on the Web site *www.ccsso.org*. Minima can be enforced against local school boards through the courts, e.g., Pittenger v. Union Area School Board, 24 Pa. Cmwlth. 442, 356 A.2d 866 (1976), or through the threat of reduction in state subsidies.

11. Even when the Report highlighted efforts in some communities

to have extended school services, it focused on extended days or ex-
tended years, but assumed the continuation of the five-day week. See
National Education Commission on Time and Learning, *Prisoners of
Time*, 35. There has been some experimentation with four-day weeks
of longer days. See Colorado Department of Education, *The Four
Day School Week* (1999) (ERIC Document Reproduction Service No.
ED429344).

12. Carl F. Kaestle, *Pillars of the Republic*, 15 (Hill and Wang, 1983).
Robert L. Church and Michael W. Sedlak, *Education in the United States*,
57 (The Free Press, 1976) offers a lower figure.

13. *Report of the Commissioner of Education 1891–92*, Vol. 2, 664.

14. Morris A. Shepard and Keith Baker, *Year-Round Schools*, 2 (D. C.
Heath, 1977); National Education Association, *A Longer School Day and
Year*, 5 (1985).

15. Shepard and Baker, *Year-Round Schools*, 1–4; National Education
Association, *A Longer School Day and Year*, 5.

16. H. G. Good, *A History of American Education*, 376 (2d ed., Macmillan,
1964). On earlier laws requiring parents and masters to educate the
young (but not requiring attendance), which had been enacted in the
seventeenth century but had long since been abrogated, see William F.
Aikman and Lawrence Kotin, *Legal Implications of Compulsory Education*,
9–23 (Mass. Center for Public Interest Law, 1976).

17. See, e.g., State v. Bailey, 157 Ind. 324, 61 N.E. 730 (1901).

18. As the Supreme Court said (long after compulsory education was
well established): "The requirement of compulsory schooling to age 16
must therefore be viewed as aimed not merely at providing educational
opportunities for children, but as an alternative to the equally undesir-
able consequence of unhealthful child labor displacing adult workers,
or, on the other hand, forced idleness." Wisconsin v. Yoder, 406 U.S. 205,
228 (1972).

19. Ch. 240, 1852 Mass. Stat., §1.

20. Ibid.

21. Ibid.

22. Ch. 42, 1860 Mass. Gen. Stat., §1.

23. Ch. 279, 1873 Mass. Stat., §1.

24. Ch. 47, 1882 Mass. Pub. Stat., §1.

25. Ch. 44, 1882 Mass. Pub. Stat., §§1 and 2.

26. Ch. 384, 1890 Mass. Stat.

27. Ibid.

28. Ch. 188, 1894 Mass. Stat.

29. Ch. 496, 1898 Mass. Stat., §§1 and 2.

30. Ch. 12, 1898 Mass. Stat.

31. Ch. 44, 1902 Mass. Rev. Laws, §1.

32. Ch. 421, 1874 N.Y. Laws 532, §1.

33. Ch. 516, 1874 Cal. Stat. 751, §1. See "An Act to Amend the Provisions of the Political Code Relative to Public Schools," 1874 Cal. Stat. 86, §61.

34. Ch. 671, 1894 N.Y. Laws 1682, §3 (Compulsory Education Law).

35. Ch. 333, 1905 Cal. Stat. 388, §1.

36. Ch. 563, 1917 N.Y. Laws 1616, §1 (urban districts); ch. 386, 1921 N.Y. Laws 1211, §621 (rural districts).

37. Ch. 487, 1921 Cal. Stat. 741, §1 (amendments to the Political Code).

38. Evidence on exactly this point is hard to find. Attendance per pupil overall rose from 78.4 days per year in 1870 to 121.2 days per year in 1921; but these figures include both rural and urban school districts. U.S. Bureau of the Census, *Historical Statistics of the United States, Colonial Times to 1970, Series H 520–530,* 375 (Kraus International Publications, 1989).

39. To what extent compulsory education laws actually caused increased school attendance (and to what extent the increase was caused by other social forces) is debatable. The sanctions of the laws, and their enforcement, became stronger starting around 1890. Good, *A History of American Education,* 378. Even before then, the laws may have had an indirect effect by stating a public standard; and there was some correlative enforcement of child labor laws which made it illegal to hire a child in the appropriate age range who had not in the last year attended school the requisite minimum number of days: e.g., Ch. 48, 1882 Mass. Pub. Stat., §2. On the joint impact of these laws, see Moses Stambler, "The Effect of Compulsory Education and Child Labor Laws on High School

Attendance in New York City, 1898–1917," *History of Education Quarterly* (Summer 1968), 189.

40. National Education Association, *A Longer School Day and Year*, 5.

41. *Report of the Commissioner of Education for 1891–92*, Vol. 2, 664–665 (1894).

42. *Report of the Commissioner of Education for 1893–94*, Vol. 1, xviii (1896).

43. Ibid., 26.

44. *Report of the Commissioner of Education for 1900–01*, Vol. 2, 1529 (1902).

45. U.S. Department of Commerce, *Historical Statistics of the United States Series H 520–530*, 375.

46. Ibid.

47. See Robert S. Brown, "The Butler Didn't Do It: An Examination of the Urban Origins of the Ontario Summer Holiday, 1846–1913," and Joel Weiss, "Telling Tales over Time: Constructing and Deconstructing the School Calendar," papers presented at the Annual Conference of the American Educational Research Association, April 22, 1999, on file with the author.

48. See National Education Association, *A Longer School Day and Year*.

49. Stanley M. Elam, Lowell C. Rose, and Alec M. Gallup, "The 23d Annual Gallup Poll of the Public's Attitudes Toward the Public Schools," 73 *Phi Delta Kappan* 41, 44–45 (September 1991); Elam, Rose, and Gallup, "The 24th Annual Gallup/Phi Delta Kappa Poll of the Public's Attitudes Toward the Public Schools," 74 *Phi Delta Kappan* 41, 49–50 (September 1992).

50. Staney M. Elam, Lowell C. Rose, and Alec M. Gallup, "The 28th Annual Phi Delta Kappa/Gallup Poll of the Public's Attitudes Toward the Public Schools," 78 *Phi Delta Kappan* 41, 52–53 (September 1996).

51. National Education Commission on Time and Learning, *Prisoners of Time*, 24.

52. Ibid., 7.

53. Michael J. Barrett, "The Case for More School Days," *The Atlantic Monthly*, November 1990, 78, 80.

54. National Education Commission on Time and Learning, *Prisoners of Time*, 34.

55. National Commission on Excellence in Education, *A Nation at Risk*, 29 (1983).

56. Compare Barrett, "The Case for More School Days," 84–86, with National Education Association, *What Research Says About: Extending the School Day/Year: Proposals and Results*, 13–15 (1987).

57. Julie Aronson, Joy Zimmerman, and Lisa Carlov, *Improving Student Achievement by Extending School: Is It Just a Matter of Time?* (WestEd, 1999) (ERIC Document Reproduction Service No. ED435127).

58. National Education Association, *What Research Says About: Extending the School Day/Year*, 6.

59. See, e.g., Susan F. Axelrad-Lentz, Michigan State Department of Education, *Michigan Extended School Year Programs 1992–1995: An Evaluation of a State Grant Initiative* (1996) (ERIC Document Reproduction Service No. ED410251); Aronson, Zimmerman, and Carlov, *Improving Student Achievement by Extending School*, 5 (Oregon adopted a plan for a longer school year in 1991, but repealed it in 1995 before implementation).

60. Council of Chief State School Officers, *Key State Education Policies on K-12 Education: 2000*, "Length of School Year."

61. Massachusetts Commission on Time and Learning, *Unlocking the Power of Time*, ii, 9–10 (1995) (recommending 190 days for students and an additional 10 paid days for development of curriculum and teachers' skills).

62. John Hodge Jones in "Epilogue" to *Prisoners of Time*, "Expanded and Updated for 2000 by Staff Development for Educators," 83 (Crystal Spring Books, 2000).

63. E. P. Thompson, "Time, Work-Discipline, and Industrial Capitalism," 38 *Past and Present* 56 (1967).

64. E.g., Michel Foucault, *Discipline and Punish*, 156ff. (Vintage Books, 2d ed., 1995).

65. For details, see Bureau of National Affairs, *Basic Patterns in Union Contracts*, 57–66 and 101–110 (14th ed., 1995).

66. Council Directive 93/104/EC, Art. 7, 1993 O.J. (L307) 18.

67. Attendance statistics are from the National Association for Year-Round Education (NAYRE) Website: *www.nayre.org/about.html#history* (10/01/01). For geographic spread, see the useful map in Elaine Warrich-

Harris, "Year-Round School: The Best Thing Since Sliced Bread," 71 *Childhood Education* 282, 283 (1995).

68. For various possible year-round plans, see Shepard and Baker, *Year-Round Schools*, 9–19, and Don Glines, *Year-Round Education: History, Philosophy, Future*, 130–151 (National Association for Year-Round Education, 1995).

69. As of 1992, all three of these plans were in use roughly equally, and much more so than any of the other alternatives. See Blaine R. Worthen and Stephen W. Zsiray, Jr., *What Twenty Years of Educational Studies Reveal About Year-Round Education*, 7 (1994) (ERIC Document Reproduction Service No. ED373413).

70. For a review of the data, see Worthen and Zsiray, *What Twenty Years of Educational Studies Reveal*, 20–22.

71. See the data in Jane L. Zykowski et al., *A Review of Year-Round Education Research*, 2–5 (California Educational Research Cooperative, 1991).

72. Statement of March 25, 1998, Los Angeles Unified School District, posted on its Web site at: *www.lausd.k12.ca.us/lausd/office_of_communications/March98c.html*.

73. Marjorie Faulstich Orellana and Barrie Thorne, "Year-Round Schools and the Politics of Time," 29 *Anthropology & Education Quarterly* 446, 455 (1998).

74. Ibid., 453.

75. Ibid., 447.

76. Worthen and Zsiray, *What Twenty Years of Educational Studies Reveal*, 10–11.

77. Zykowski et al., *A Review of Year-Round Education Research*, iv. A further study to the same effect is Robert B. Pittman and Mary Jean Ronan Herzog, "Evaluation of a Year-Round Schedule in a Rural School District," 14 *Journal of Research in Rural Education* no. 1, 15–16 (Spring 1998). For a study suggesting that if the adoption of year-round education leads teachers to rethink what they are doing, it can lead to improved academic achievement, see Carolyn M. Shields and Steven L. Oberg, "What Can We Learn From The Data? Toward a Better Understanding of the Effects of Multitrack Year-Round Schooling," 34 *Urban Education* no. 2, 125 (May 1999).

78. For a similar conclusion reached with regard to one particular implementation of a year-round schedule, see Joan L. Herman, "Novel Approaches to Relieve Overcrowding," 26 *Urban Education* 195 (1991).

79. Glines, *Year-Round Education*, 119–120.

80. See Orellana and Thorne, "Year-Round Schools and the Politics of Time," 467.

81. Zykowski et al., *A Review of Year-Round Education Research*, 39. Some school districts have, however, been forced by public opinion to give up on year-round experiments. Linda Rodgers, "The Pros and Cons of Year-Round Education at the Elementary Public School Level," 33 (1993) (thesis; ERIC Document Reproduction Service No. ED370160).

82. *Report of the Commissioner of Education, 1891–92*, Vol. 2, 664. See also William A. Cook, *High School Administration*, 140–143 (Warwick & York, 1926).

83. For the latest requirements, see Council of Chief State School Officers, *Key State Education Policies on K–12 Education* (2000).

84. National Education Commission on Time and Learning, *Prisoners of Time*, 34; Massachusetts Commission on Time and Learning, *Time for Change*, 7 (1994).

85. Stanley M. Elam, Lowell C. Rose, and Alec M. Gallup, "The 25th Annual Phi Delta Kappa/Gallup Poll of the Public's Attitudes Toward the Public Schools," 75 *Phi Delta Kappan* 137, 147–148 (October 1993).

6. Disputes at the Boundaries of Time

1. See Todd D. Rakoff, "Implied Terms: Of 'Default Rules' and 'Situation Sense,'" in Jack Beatson and Daniel Friedmann, eds., *Good Faith and Fault in Contract Law* (Oxford University Press, 1995).

2. This was the situation faced by Johanna Upton when her employer demanded an extraordinary amount of overtime, in the case described at the beginning of Chapter 4.

3. Bureau of National Affairs, *Basic Patterns in Union Contracts*, 7 (14th ed., 1995).

4. James R. Redeker, *Discipline: Policies and Procedures*, 55–69 (Bureau of National Affairs, 1983).

5. Tim Bornstein et al., *Labor and Employment Arbitration*, Vol. I, §17.01[3][a] (Matthew Bender, 2001) (on-line); In re National-Standard Co., 79 Lab. Arb. Rep. (BNA) 837 (1982); In re Velva Sheen Manuf. Co., 98 Lab. Arb. Rep. (BNA) 741 (1992); In re Southwestern Bell Telephone Co., 114 Lab. Arb. Rep. (BNA) 1131 (2000).

6. See generally Bornstein et al., *Labor and Employment Arbitration*, Vol. I, §17.02.

7. For examples, see the plans described in In re Schuller International, Inc., 107 Lab. Arb. Rep. (BNA) 1109 (1996), and in In re Armstrong World Industries, Inc., 109 Lab. Arb. Rep. (BNA) 65 (1997).

8. In re Georgia-Pacific Corporation, 108 Lab. Arb. Rep. (BNA) 438, 439 (1997).

9. In re Armstrong World Industries, Inc., 109 Lab. Arb. Rep. (BNA) 65, 69 (1997); accord, In re Cutler-Hammer/Eaton Corp., 113 Lab. Arb. Rep. (BNA) 409, 414 (1999).

10. In re Georgia-Pacific Corporation, 108 Lab. Arb. Rep. (BNA) 438 (1997). Accord, e.g.: In re Missouri Gas Energy, 110 Lab. Arb. Rep. (BNA) 164 (1998) (no-fault scheme legitimate but procedural faults in application); In re National Gypsum Co., 112 Lab. Arb. Rep. 248 (1999).

11. Resolving the tension between "management rights" and "just cause" provisions is an issue that is within the hands of arbitrators, not courts. E.g., Midwest Coca-Cola Bottling Co. v. Allied Sales Drivers, etc., Union, 89 F.3d 514 (8th Cir. 1996).

12. In re Safeway Stores, Inc., 79 Lab. Arb. Rep. (BNA) 742 (1982).

13. In re Velva Sheen Manuf. Co., 98 Lab. Arb. Rep. (BNA) 741 (1992), supports a similar analysis.

14. Annotation, "Discharge for Absenteeism or Tardiness As Affecting Right to Unemployment Compensation," 58 A.L.R.3d 674, §3 (1974 and Supp. 2001).

15. E.g., Lycurgus v. Director of Division of Employment Security, 391 Mass. 623, 462 N.E.2d 326 (1984); Evenson v. Omnetic's, 344 N.W.2d 881 (Minn. App. 1984); In re Claim of Ulin E. Lewis, 244 A.D.2d 750, 664 N.Y.S.2d 668 (1997).

16. E.g., Gonzales v. Industrial Commission, 740 P.2d 999 (Colo. 1987; Mannor Corp. v. Sanders, 624 So.2d 617 (Ala. Civ. App. 1993); Garden

View Care Center, Inc. v. Labor and Industrial Relations Commission, 848 S.W.2d 603 (Mo. App. 1993).

17. Annotation, "Discharge for Absenteeism or Tardiness As Affecting Right to Unemployment Compensation," 58 A.L.R.3d 674 (1974 and Supp. 2001), §§14(b) and 15(b).

18. Ibid., §§14(a) and 15(a).

19. See the beginning of Chapter 4.

20. Bureau of National Affairs, *Basic Patterns in Union Contracts,* 50–51.

21. Michael L. Smith, "Mandatory Overtime and Quality of Life in the 1990s," 21 *Journal of Corporation Law* 599, 612 (1996); Roger I. Abrams and Dennis R. Nolan, "Time at a Premium: The Arbitration of Overtime and Premium Pay Disputes," 45 *Ohio State Law Journal* 837, 845 (1984); Bornstein et al., *Labor and Employment Arbitration,* Vol. II, §33.04.

22. Smith, "Mandatory Overtime and Quality of Life," 613; Abrams and Nolan, "Time at a Premium," 845.

23. In re Ford Motor Co., 11 Lab. Arb. Rep. (BNA) 1158, 1160 (1948).

24. E.g., In re Sonoco Products Co., 107 Lab. Arb. Rep. (BNA) 782 (1996) (suspension upheld; notice given at 2:40 P.M. of overtime that evening; employee claim of "I have an appointment" not adequate excuse).

25. See In re Hygrade Food Products Co., 69 Lab. Arb. Rep. (BNA) 414 (1977) ("sore ankles" would have been excuse from further work standing in the cold, but not shown).

26. In re Lear Seating Corp., 98 Lab. Arb. Rep. (BNA) 194 (1991).

27. In re Ford Motor Co., 11 Lab. Arb. Rep. (BNA) 1158 (1948).

28. In re Piedmont Airlines, Inc., 103 Lab. Arb. Rep. (BNA) 751 (1994).

29. Martin H. Malin, "Fathers and Parental Leave Revisited," 19 *Northern Illinois University Law Review* 25, 42–44 (1998), takes the position that the Piedmont Airlines case represents a minority view among arbitrators. As discussed earlier, it is very hard to establish what the dominant view of arbitrators is; even if Malin were correct, it is surely true that the case represents at least a well-established view, and one that is more indicative of the overall balance of the law once at-will relationships are taken into account. But Malin's interpretation is doubtful

because he only cites older authority (see ibid., n. 104) and does not explain his understanding of the more recent cases.

30. In re Ashland Oil, Inc., 91 Lab. Arb. Rep. (BNA) 1101 (1988).

31. Ibid., 1104.

32. In re Southern Champion Tray Co., 96 Lab. Arb. Rep. (BNA) 633, 637 (1991).

33. Smith, "Mandatory Overtime and Quality of Life," 616–621.

34. Arizona Department of Economic Security v. Valdez, 119 Ariz. 570, 582 P.2d 660 (Ct. App. 1978); quotation at 582 P.2d at 662.

35. Smith, "Mandatory Overtime and Quality of Life," 621; see, e.g., Jones v. Pa. Unemployment Compensation Board of Review, 98 Pa. Commw. 246, 510 A.2d 1278 (1986).

36. On time use as signaling social priority, see Robert Levine, *The Geography of Time,* 101ff. (Basic Books, 1997).

37. On the substitution of TV watching for participatory activity, see Robert Putnam's Foreword to John P. Robinson and Geoffrey Godbey, *Time for Life,* xiii (Pennsylvania State University Press, 2d ed., 1997), and the further comments on p. 344.

38. In re General Cable Corp., 15 Lab. Arb. Rep. (BNA) 910, 912 (1950).

39. In re Belcor, Inc., 77 Lab. Arb. Rep. (BNA) 23, 26 (1981).

40. Frank Elkouri and Edna Asper Elkouri, *How Arbitration Works,* ed. Martin M. Wolz and Edward P. Goggin, 725–732 (Bureau of National Affairs, 1997).

41. Prickett v. Circuit Science, Inc., 499 N.W.2d 506, 508 (Minn. App., 1993); accord, White v. Security Link, 658 A.2d 619 (Del. Super., 1994); see Annotation, "Unemployment Compensation: Eligibility as Affected by Claimant's Refusal To Work at Particular Times or on Particular Shifts for Domestic or Family Reasons," 2 A.L.R.5th 475 (1992 and Supp. 2001).

42. Newland v. Job Service North Dakota, 460 N.W.2d 118 (1990).

43. Mont. Code Ann. §39-2-901 et seq. (2001).

44. 29 U.S.C. §2601 et seq. (2000).

45. Ibid., §2601(a)(3).

46. Ibid., §2601(b)(1).

47. Ibid., §2612(a)(1) and (2).

48. Ibid., §2611(2) and (4).

49. Ibid., §2612(c) and (d).

50. Ibid., §2612(a)(1).

51. Ibid., §2615(a)(1).

52. Ibid., §2617.

53. Ibid., §2614.

54. For an overall picture of the situation, see Marc Linder, *Moments Are the Elements of Profit,* 186ff. (Fanpihua Press, 2000).

55. Maine Rev. Stat. Ann., Title 26, §603 (Supp. 2001).

56. Linder, *Moments Are the Elements of Profit,* 194–198 (discussing origins of the Act in conditions at the Poland Springs bottling plant).

57. Lisa L. Tharpe, "Analysis of the Political Dynamics Surrounding the Enactment of the 1993 Family and Medical Leave Act," 47 *Emory Law Journal* 379, 394ff. (1998).

58. See Arlie Hochschild, *The Time Bind,* 27 and footnote (Henry Holt, 1997); see also Barbara Kate Repa, "The Family and Medical Leave Act: Is It Lip Service Leave?" (Nolo Press, *www.nolo.com/Chunkemp/family leave.html*) (11/6/98).

59. For further discussion of the possible advantages of giving employees rather than employers the right to make decisions (or the power to bargain away that right), see Cass Sunstein, "Human Behavior and the Law of Work," 87 *Virginia Law Review* 205 (2001)—which, however, emphasizes cognitive difficulties more, and social pressures less, than the argument presented here.

60. H.R.1, 105th Cong. (1st Sess. 1997) ("Working Families Flexibility Act of 1997"); S.4, 105th Cong. (1st Sess. 1997) ("Family Friendly Workplace Act"); H.R.1380, 106th Cong. (1st Sess. 1999) ("Working Families Flexibility Act of 1999"); S.624, 107th Cong. (1st Sess. 2001) ("Workplace Flexibility Act"); H.R.1982, 107th Cong. (1st Sess. 2001) ("Working Families Flexibility Act of 2001").

61. 29 U.S.C. §207(o) (2000).

62. H.R. Rep. 105-21, 195th Cong., 1st Sess (1997).

63. Ibid., 3, reporting amended H.R.1, §2(r)(7) (105th Cong., 1st Sess.).

64. Thus the proposal would not have been subject to the problem regarding public comptime which later was the subject of the Supreme Court's decision in Christensen v. Harris County, 529 U.S. 576 (2000).

65. H.R. Rep. 105-21, 195th Cong., 1st Sess. (1997).

66. Ibid., 37.

67. Sen. Rep. 105-11, 105th Cong., 1st Sess., 6–7 (1997).

68. Lonnie Golden, "Timing is Everything: Potential Economic Repercussions of Proposed 'Flextime' Reforms to the FLSA Overtime Hours Law," *Labor Law Journal* 504, 507 (August 1997).

69. David J. Walsh, "The FLSA Comp Time Controversy: Fostering Flexibility or Diminishing Worker Rights?" 20 *Berkeley Journal of Employment and Labor Law* 74, 99–101 (1999).

70. See ibid., 101–102.

71. S.4, 105th Cong. (1st Sess 1997); S.624, 107th Cong. (1st Sess. 2001).

72. S.4, 105th Cong. (1st Sess. 1997), 33.

7. THE GENERAL CASE

1. See David P. Currie, "The Sunday Mails," 2 *The Green Bag* 361 (2d series, 1999).

2. See Gary S. Becker, "A Theory of the Allocation of Time," 75 *The Economic Journal* 493 (1965).

3. See Milton Friedman, *Capitalism and Freedom*, chap. 1 (University of Chicago Press, 1962) and Michael J. Trebilcock, *The Limits of Freedom of Contract*, chap. 1 (Harvard University Press, 1993).

4. Juliet Schor, *The Overworked American*, 43ff. (Basic Books, 1993).

5. Max Weber, *The Protestant Ethic and the Spirit of Capitalism* (trans. T. Parsons; Charles Scribner's Sons, 1958).

6. See Michael Walzer, "The Communitarian Critique of Liberalism," 18 *Political Theory* 6, 11–12 (1990).

7. Alexis de Tocqueville, *Democracy in America*, 509ff. (ed. J. P. Mayer; Anchor Books, 1969); Robert D. Putnam, *Bowling Alone*, 15ff. (Simon and Schuster, 2000).

8. William H. McNeill, *Keeping Together in Time* (Harvard University Press, 1995).

9. Emile Durkheim, *The Elementary Forms of Religious Life*, 8–10 (trans. K. Fields; The Free Press, 1995); Pitirim A. Sorokin, *Sociocultural Causality, Space, Time*, 172–173 (Duke University Press, 1943); Eviatar Zerubavel, *Hidden Rhythms*, 64–67 (University of California Press, 1985);

Eviatar Zerubavel, *The Seven Day Circle,* 22–23 (University of Chicago Press, 1989).

10. See the discussion in Chapter 4.

11. On the interplay of time and money as modes of political participation, see generally Sidney Verba, Kay Lehman Schlozman, and Henry E. Brady, *Voice and Equality* (Harvard University Press, 1995).

12. Robert D. Putnam, "Bowling Alone: America's Declining Social Capital," 6 *Journal of Democracy* 65, 71 (1995).

13. See Murray Melbin, "Night as Frontier," 43 *American Sociological Review* 3 (1978).

14. See David Harvey, *The Condition of Postmodernity,* 284ff. (Blackwell, 1990).

15. I am putting to one side any question of whether the individual negotiators in this matter accurately reflect the purely social goods involved. We may assume, to simplify the matter, that each individual in the society includes within his or her own desires the necessary other-regarding preferences to make this happen; that parents, for example, value their own membership in coherent families and also value providing that opportunity for their children.

16. See the discussion in Chapter 6.

17. Ecclesiastes 3:1 (Revised Standard Version). Seeger's song is entitled "Turn, Turn, Turn," and he used the phraseology of the King James Version: "A time *to* every purpose."

INDEX